of us are unsure as to what we will find when we cross over. So many are afraid. So many have no belief, and some think only the 'select few' will go somewhere positive. Mark Macy's book alleviates fear and doubt and opens the way to inner peace while living on earth. This book can encourage all to live in harmony and to respect one another.

"In these times when there are so many wars and so much fear and terrorism, it is work like Mark Macy's that can encourage all to put away weapons of war, to put away feelings of hostility and anger toward one another, and to replace them with respect, honesty, and peace. Knowing that life goes on after death may be the key factor in bringing humankind together."

—Dr. Marilyn Rossner, Ph.D, EdD Special Education; Behavior therapist; Yoga therapist and World Renowned Medium and Intuitive; Vice President, IIIHS (International Institute for Integral Human Studies); Founder and President, Spiritualist Science Fellowship

SPIRIT FACES

TRUTH ABOUT THE AFTERLIFE

Mark Macy

WEISER BOOKS
San Francisco, CA / Newburyport, MA

First published in 2006 by Red Wheel/Weiser, LLC
With offices at:
500 Third Street, Suite 230
San Francisco, CA 94107
www.redwheelweiser.com

ISBN-10: 1-57863-381-8
ISBN-13: 978-1-57863-381-4

Library of Congress Cataloging-in-Publication Data

Macy, Mark, 1949–
  Spirit faces : truth about the afterlife / Mark Macy.
      p. cm.
  ISBN 1-57863-381-8 (alk. paper)
  1. Spiritualism. 2. Future life. I. Title.
  BF1261.2.M325 2006
  133.9--dc22

                                          2006011580

Cover and text design by Donna Linden.
Typeset in Berkeley and Copperplate.
Cover photograph © Mark Macy.

Printed in Hong Kong
SS
10 9 8 7 6 5 4 3 2 1

CONTENTS

ACKNOWLEDGMENTS

I owe a big debt of gratitude to my wife and twin soul Regina for her support and encouragement during these fifteen years of research, a time of tremendous gratification for both of us. Like any new frontier, we encountered frustration and, well, weirdness at times, but we remained a cohesive team through it all.

My eternal gratitude goes to The Seven ethereal beings for sticking with us humans, waiting patiently for us to see the light, and providing guidance and support down through the ages. Also to our many ancestors and departed loved ones who, after settling in finer spiritual realms, still choose to help us out here on this troubled little planet as it spins through physical space. They are far too numerous to list, but those who have touched my life personally in a big way through extraordinary ITC contacts include Konstantin Raudive, Arthur Beckwith, and Bill O'Neil.

Colleagues in this world to whom I owe a debt of gratitude are also numerous, but those who really changed my life are George Meek, the teacher who came along when this student was ready; and Maggy and Jules Harsch-Fischbach, who allowed me into their private world of soul-stirring miracles to share the awe while spreading the word.

I'm sure our spirit friends share my gratitude for the tireless efforts of Rolf Ehrhardt and Hans Heckmann. Rolf forged the vessel of worlditc.org by building a formidable website, and he has kept it on course—toward resonance—through the storms. Hans labored selflessly to translate world-changing ITC contacts from German to English that will set fire to minds throughout the world in the coming years.

And finally, to those spirit friends who made the pictures possible for this book, especially my father (Blair Macy) and Regina's dad (John Hoys), John Denver, Robert Monroe, Albert Einstein, Edgar Cayce, Willis Harman, John Alberti, William Dubs, and, last but not least, Buddy the German shepherd. To them and to the thousands of other spirits whose faces we've not yet recognized: Thank you all so much!

Foreword

※

*Since the early 1990s, Mark Macy has been talking to the so-called
dead. Now he is taking their pictures.*

When I grew up, one picture was worth a thousand words.
The local dairy even advertised that "seeing is believing; that's
why we use glass bottles." So, in the sixties, when words finally
failed to even *begin* to describe what was happening in this
country, some of us picked up cameras and took to the streets.
We did our own research into what was true—first, with 35mm
still, then with 16mm movie cameras. This was photography as
verification, as evidence, as proof. And not just pointed at
policemen or civil unrest. Ours was an earnest exploration into
reality itself, into humanity, consciousness, being, and light. We
fell in love with light.

Too soon then, film gave way to videotape and video went
to digital, now digital is on its way to God Knows Where, and
the practice of photography has shifted from an interest in *what
is* to whatever can be made to *appear to be*. It's all about manip-
ulation now. Trucks morph into robots, into football players,

helicopters, automatic weapons fire, incoming asteroids, giant pills. The very glint in the eye of the celebrity starlet is routinely plucked from its socket, its pixels altered, then popped back in, all for the sake of sales.

Mark Macy's luminator photographs are something else. His book, *Spirit Faces: Truth About the Afterlife,* is his report on research into reality itself, into humanity, consciousness, being and life on both sides of the veil. It is photography as verification, as evidence, as proof.

Fifteen years ago, Macy found himself drawn into the work of instrumental transcommunication (ITC), which had been going on quietly since the 1950s, mostly in Europe, he writes. ITC is "the use of TVs, radios, telephones, computers, and other technical devices to get information from the spirit worlds in the form of voices, images, and text."

ITC has been talking to spirits.

In *Conversations Beyond the Light* (written with Dr. Pat Kubis), Macy documents electronic communications between ITC communicators in this world and their spirit colleagues in the next. Some of what's been learned is that

> ... the physical universe is but a small part of creation,
> that all worlds throughout this immense universe are
> composed of pure consciousness, and that the number
> one law of life everywhere is: Thoughts create reality.

What separates these worlds one from another is the difference in the frequency at which their matter vibrates. This is what Itzhak Bentov says, and Drunvalo Melchizedek, and A.E. Powell, as well as paranormal investigator George W. Meek (*After We Die, What Then?*), who brought Macy into ITC before his death in 1999, agree. In 1991, Meek told Macy:

> You know this room is filled with radio signals, right?
> And you know that each signal remains distinct by its
> frequency. That's why a radio can tune separately to each

signal. Well, all the spiritual universes—and there are hundreds of them—they're all sharing this space with our physical universe, like radio signals sharing the room.

In *Miracles in the Storm* (2001), Macy continues:

The room is also filled with many types of invisible beings, from ghosts to angels, that move in and out of our lives everyday. Those which have the most profound effect on us are those who resonate with our thoughts, feelings, and attitudes. People on Earth draw into their lives spirit beings of like attitude.

While I was in the process of writing about ITC for my book, *People Who Don't Know They're Dead,* my uncle Wally Johnston emailed me about a workshop scheduled at the Edgar Cayce ARE Center in New York. Mark Macy would be there with his luminator machine. He would be taking pictures. I went and he was.

I liked Mark immediately—electric sky blue eyes, soft-spoken, sincere. He spoke from index cards. I got a good vibe.

Mark didn't say exactly how his luminator works. In fact, he may not know. What he does know is that sometimes when he turns it on and takes a Polaroid picture, faces of beings other than those who are posing for the photograph appear on film. The *subtle energy field* produced by the luminator seems somehow to help increase the density of otherwise invisible beings to the point where they bounce light; enough light to expose an image on film.

Mark uses an off-the-shelf Polaroid 600 and stock film. His only modification to the camera is a piece of tape placed over the flash bar with a hole cut in it the size of a sesame seed.

One of the stand-out subjects in *Spirit Faces* is Debbie Alberti. Debbie sought Mark out. After reading his books and plumbing his website, Debbie showed up at the workshop and

Mark took several pictures. In the third one, clearly superimposed over Debbie's lower face and throat, appeared the face of her husband, John. John had been dead nine weeks. Debbie was ecstatic.

As with the other two to three thousand pictures he has taken since the fall of '99, Mark knows that the natural human reaction is that it's most likely faked. Adobe Photoshop or any number of other computer techniques could create such an image, and there is no other way earthly physics can explain such a thing. But, Mark writes

> . . . based on *spirit-world physics,* that picture *is* possible, and I know for certain that it's a legitimate spirit picture. So do the six people in that New York City workshop who witnessed the untouched photo as it developed.

I was one of the six people at that workshop. I saw Mark take Debbie's picture, and I watched the untouched photograph develop.

It happened.

A year later, in June of 2005, Weiser Books publisher Jan Johnson and I met with Mark at his lab outside Boulder, Colorado. I had been urging Jan to publish Mark's pictures. Pictures were taken. In one, the face of a bearded man superimposed itself over Jan Johnson's face. In a series of photos, a familiar face rose over my shoulder, looking like a Chinese woman, or possibly my aunt; in fact, considering a certain family resemblance, it could have been my own astral body adrift.

Something or someone invisible to the three of us in that room, between the subject of the photo and the film in Mark's camera, had bounced enough light to register an image.

Five months after that, when I returned on my own, the face of a dog looking very much like my German shepherd, dead 20 years, superimposed itself over my lower face and throat. (See photos 1 and 2, Gary.)

Mark regards the luminator images as

> . . . a gift given to me by "the powers that be," with the understanding that I don't just display them as paranormal phenomena, but instead use them as a tool to help spread spiritual understanding. So I use the images as solid evidence—verifiable proof of the worlds of spirit—upon which to build a stable model of spiritual reality.

Spirit Faces is the revelation and exploration of that spiritual model, both a recognition of the gift and a challenge to the reader to hold up our end of the bargain.

ITC's contacts with the other side are the fruits of no small effort. According to Mark, they are the result of intensive spirit-world planning and choreography.

> Our spirit group has to come close to our world in vibration, locate us in time and space, and then make the contact—a very difficult feat, we are told.

And only possible "when the vibrations of those present are in complete harmony, and when their aims and intentions are pure," Konstantin Raudive told the group in Luxembourg through radio sounds from the other side in the summer of 1994.

The too human traits of envy, cynicism, competition, fear, and doubt amongst ITC researchers on this side slowed communications to a trickle in 2000. ITC's spirit colleagues pulled out of the conversation.

Mark hopes that these luminator pictures signal a willingness on the part of spirit communicators to rebuild the conscious bridge between worlds, but

> Good communication across the veil . . . depends on resonance of minds . . . an opening of the heart on the part of the folks at both ends of the line—an acknowledgement of each other's being and a sincere concern for each other.

Spirit Faces is full of wisdom. It's an important book. Mark Macy is for real. The universe is large, all worlds within it are composed of pure consciousness, and the number one law everywhere is:

Thoughts create reality.

The essence of reality is vibration. We literally attract our lives. People draw into their lives spirit beings of like attitude. The responsibility is ours.

> Love and empathy expressed by people on Earth are fueled by the support of loving and empathetic spirit beings. Conversely, resentment and fear felt by individuals on Earth are fueled by eager support of negative spirits.

Take a look.

Gary Leon Hill,
author of *People Who Don't Know They're Dead*

AUTHOR'S NOTE

Gary Hill attended my workshop at the Edgar Cayce ARE (Association for Research and Enlightenment) Center in New York City on May 14, 2004, and seemed intrigued as the miraculous photo of Debbie and John Alberti was taken and developed before his eyes. Not long afterwards, he had the original brainstorm for a book about these spirit faces, and he kindled an interest with his publisher and with me.

Gary visited my lab a year before the book was published, and we got some good spirit faces during his visit. One of the more pleasantly surprising moments I've had during my work came as I watched a picture of Gary developing, and I thought I saw the contented face of a dog emerging in the picture, at Gary's throat (photos 1 and 2, Gary).

I asked Gary, "Did you ever have a German shepherd?"

Gary's eyes widened as he took the picture and began to study it. He exclaimed, "That's Buddy!"

Buddy was a German shepherd who shared Gary's loft apartment in Manhattan for a number of years. The dog has been long dead, but he appeared with a wise and peaceful look on his face that day in my lab.

My wife, our son Aaron, and I had owned two pet cats, Konrad and Sebastian, and I had tried on numerous occasions to get pictures of them after they'd died, with no success. I know from other experiences in my research that cats, dogs, and other beloved animals often share our afterlife experience. When they die, they live on in the same spirit worlds as our late loved ones and are there to greet us when we ourselves cross over. So I suspected it was possible to capture their images on film. At last that was confirmed.

Thanks, Buddy.

INTRODUCTION

We each view the worlds of spirit in our own personal way—through religion, paranormal research, new-age philosophy, science fiction, meditation, or agnosticism. In our mind those invisible realms might be a place of heaven and hell, of ghosts and hauntings, of vast powers and energies that we can tap into in order to transform our lives and our world, of extraterrestrials, of angels and demons, of ancestors, or of divine inspiration. Or the spirit worlds might be all in our mind, period.

My research suggests that the spirit worlds are all of these things and more.

This book is mostly about some unusual Polaroid pictures that I take in my lab and on the road while giving seminars and workshops. They are made possible in part by a machine called a *luminator*. When I take pictures of people in the presence of the luminator, I often get other faces in the pictures—faces of people who are not physically present—what I call *spirit faces*. They are often as natural and solid looking as the human face in the picture, but they clearly belong to someone else. Sometimes they are nearly transparent. While many of the faces are blurry, some are so clear that you can almost feel the personality and mood of the spirit person.

The presence of these spirit faces on film raises many questions: Are they in what is called *the afterlife?* If so, how can they be right here among us at the same time? Where exactly is the afterlife? Do these invisible people affect us? If so, is their influence beneficial or harmful? What can we gain from being aware of these invisible people? Can we communicate with them? Would that be a good thing or a bad thing to do? Or is my basic assumption incorrect—the assumption that these are spirit faces? Are there other possible explanations? Those questions and many others are explored in this book.

I regard the luminator images as a sort of gift given to me by the powers that be, with the understanding that I don't just display them as paranormal phenomena, but also use them as a tool to help spread spiritual understanding. So I use the images as solid evidence—veritable proof of the worlds of spirit—upon which to build a stable model of spiritual reality.

The photos are part of the growing research called *instrumental transcommunication,* or ITC, which is the use of TVs, radios, telephones, computers, and other technical devices to get information from the spirit worlds in the form of voices, images, and text. ITC has been going on quietly since the 1950s, mostly in Europe, and will soon break out everywhere, transforming our world into a spiritual paradise as it opens broader frontiers of science than we have seen for thousands of years. I know this to be true from what I have witnessed during my past fifteen years of close collaboration with researchers from around the world, and beyond.

This book includes, along with the luminator images, a small sampling of more elaborate spirit contacts received by experimenters around the world through various forms of technical equipment.[1] The spirit-world descriptions throughout the book

---

[1] Most of those contacts were received by Maggy Harsch-Fishbach of Luxembourg. They were translated into English by Hans Heckmann, and I included them in the journals *Contact!* and *Transdimension,* which I published between 1995 and 2000. These journals can be seen on my Web site, www.spiritfaces.com.

are based on actual reports that I've collected during my fifteen years of research. As for the various spirit beings mentioned by name in this book, researchers have received actual contacts from or images of or reports about all of them. A group of ethereal beings calling themselves *The Seven* shared soul-stirring insights with us. We received a report about the experiences of Swedish Prime Minister Olof Palme after his assassination. A Native American elder named Red Jacket delivered a report to us through our spirit team. John Denver showed himself in a Polaroid picture. We received reports of several people having some difficult times once they crossed over, including Pope Pius IX, Auschwitz commandant Rudolf Hoess, an American celebrity to whom I refer simply as W, and a German soldier named Arthur M. We've received fascinating messages from a Viking poet named Skjoldung, an island girl named Mootai, an ancient Chinese physician named Yang Fudse, and an African scout named Bwele M'Banga, indicating that ITC is a project destined to encompass all mankind, not just a few researchers or a few cultures. Researchers have received works of art and information from Susannah Lehnhoff (wife of artist Edouard Manet) and Honorine Deviane (wife of author Jules Verne), and from scientists Thomas Edison, Albert Einstein, Marie Curie, and Henri Sainte-Claire de Ville, as well as from Hollywood filmmakers George Cukor and Hal Roach. Except for The Seven, these are all people who once lived on earth and who now are alive and well and communicating with us from the worlds of spirit.

The more we become involved in spiritual matters, the more apparent it is that our physical minds and bodies are just temporary vehicles in which our spirit—our true self—can navigate this dense and troubled planet. I know from personal experience that the more we know about the wonders of the afterlife, the more lightly we tread on the earth. Without that knowledge there is in many people a desperation to stuff more, more, more worldly things into our lives, usually at the expense of the people, plants, animals, and environments around us. An inner knowledge of our rich spiritual heritage allows us to relax and enjoy life on earth more fully than otherwise possible.

PART ONE

A GLIMPSE AT THE OTHER SIDE

We sometimes wake up from a dream with vivid images of other-worldly scenarios, but those dream images quickly fade away as our conscious mind kicks in.

Sometimes we see a shadowy movement out of the corner of our eye, but when we turn our head, there's nothing there.

Sometimes we hear fleeting voices, but since we're all alone, we decide that the voices are all in our head.

Sometimes we get impressions, insights, and powerful gut feelings that simply amaze us, and we're rather impressed that we can be so smart and insightful.

Many strange things happen to us from day to day, and we like to try to explain them away with common sense and scientific understanding.

But sometimes that worldly wisdom is not enough, and we have to explore other-worldly scenarios.

CHAPTER ONE

※

MORE TO LIFE THAN MEETS THE EYE

Colon cancer nearly killed me in 1988. Until that point I was agnostic; I didn't believe in God or ghosts or an afterlife. But with death staring me in the face, and suddenly gripped by fear, I gradually became consumed by the question of what really happens to us after we die. At some level I knew that the answer was the only thing that would alleviate my fears.

Over nearly two decades answers came to me in a most amazing way, and that's what this book is about: the truth about other-worldly reality as I found it—a truth based not on faith or belief, but on objective evidence. Not that there's anything wrong with faith. It's just that I was born with a curious mind that has always needed proof. What I share with you in this book is the fruit of my search—a glimpse into a much grander, much more exciting and wonderful reality than most of us on earth would normally imagine—a more profound existence than we could ever hope to understand or experience while wearing our physical bodies. It is an existence we can't know until we begin to explore beyond the limits of these bodies through such means as meditation, esoteric teachings, and ITC research. This book is all about breaking through our limitations.

There's a lot I don't yet fully understand about spiritual existence, but I do know this:

- The part of reality that we perceive with our senses and sciences is like a grain of sand on a beach. Most of reality is imperceptible to us.
- Our understanding of the bigger picture begins where our earthly lives end. The larger truth is summed up in what we sometimes call *the afterlife*.
- Our physical body is like a shroud over our mind, severely limiting the mind's view. When the physical body dies, our mind lives on with a view of far greater depth and clarity.
- Still, many of the patterns we've established on earth—patterns of thinking, patterns of behaving—we bring many of these with us to the next life, so that in many ways "life goes on" as usual after we die.

I know these things because since 1992 I have been immersed in a form of high-tech spiritual research called ITC, the use of technology to get in touch directly with the worlds of spirit. I've talked on the phone with people who died years earlier. I've heard their voices come through radios. I have colleagues in Europe who leave for work in the morning, making sure that everything at home is turned off, but sometimes they get home in the evening to find a computer running and new files planted on the disk by invisible hands. The files might contain text, or they might contain images—pictures of actual faces and places in the spirit worlds. I have other colleagues who capture spirit faces flashing across their TV screens. I have an audiocassette containing a long message, in English, from an ethereal being describing our ancient heritage, which began long before recorded history.

This book focuses on a small but important subset of ITC—the images I receive in the presence of a luminator—but it also weaves in many of the other-worldly insights I've gained over the years through the broader field of ITC research. In my other writing, especially on my original Web site, I explore the diverse field of ITC in more depth. When I started www.worlditc.org in 1998, I had no idea that it would evolve into the vast treasure chest of spiritual information that it has become thanks mostly to my good friend Rolf Ehrhardt of Ratingen, Germany, who joined forces with me in 2002. The most compelling ITC results have come out of Europe, and most of it was documented in German. Since retiring from applied physics, Rolf spends much of his time tirelessly researching ITC. He has gathered good ITC information from researchers around the world, arranged for much of the best European ITC literature to be translated into English, and posted it all on our Web site.

The coming chapters take a close look at the images of people from invisible worlds, describe those worlds and their inhabitants in some detail, and offer tips on how to invite mostly positive, loving spiritual influences into our lives and into our world.

One of the first pictures I received in the presence of the luminator contained faces of Blair Macy (my father) and Willis Harman (president of the Institute of Noetic Sciences). Both men had died a few years earlier and were especially intrigued by my research.

In the fall of 1999, my friend and colleague Jack Stucki was visiting my experimental team as we met in my lab soliciting radio contacts. We took two breaks for photos. When Jack took a picture of me, the face in the resulting photo looked vaguely familiar to me as I studied it with a magnifying glass (photos 3 and 4, Mark).

One member of our team, Judy, asked, "Is it your father?"

As soon as she said it, I recognized Dad.

But when my wife Regina glanced at the picture, she said, "It looks like Willis Harman." While Regina had seen pictures of Willis, she had never met him, so I discounted that possibility. But as I studied the picture I realized there were actually two half-faces making up the face—my father on the left and someone else on the right. I thought, "You know, that *could* be Willis Harman."

A few days later I delivered the photo to a photo studio and had several copies and reverse copies made. I cut one copy and one reverse in half down the middle of the face (photos 5 and 6, Mark), and I fit the two mirror images together to form two composite faces (photos 7 and 8, Mark) that bore a striking resemblance to the two men in lifetime (photos 9, Blair, and 10, Willis). My mother immediately recognized my father when I showed her that composite image (photo 7, Mark), and Willis's wife, Charlene, recognized her late husband the moment she saw the original image (photos 3 and 4, Mark).

CHAPTER TWO

❧

WHERE ARE THE SPIRIT WORLDS?

This book is mostly about invisible people (spirits) who inhabit invisible worlds, who frequently move in and out of our world, and who become visible under the right conditions, such as the Polaroid pictures taken in the presence of the luminator. When they come to pose with us in our pictures, where do they come from?

A businessman moved his business across town, and he decided to throw an open house for his customers. On the big day, the wine, the cheese, and the flowers all arrived, but the flowers had a banner across the front that said, "Rest in Peace." Meanwhile, somewhere across town there was a funeral underway, and the banner on one immense bouquet said, "Good luck in your new location!"

After we die and move to a new location, where exactly are we? Oddly enough, we're just a breath away from our loved ones on earth, and at the same time worlds away, out of reach. Physical existence and spiritual existence together compose an enigma. It's like asking a traveler who's getting off the phone with his family, "How close are you to your family?" The traveler might reply that his wife and kids are thousands of miles away, or he might tap his chest and say, "They're right here." That's how it is with the afterlife.

Radio and TV signals fill the room we are in right now, and if our eyes and ears were built a little differently, we would actually be able to see and hear them, just the way we can see sunbeams stream through the window onto the furniture and the way we can hear the cat purring on our lap. If we could see and hear the radio and TV signals all around us, we would be overwhelmed by the many songs, the personalities, and the comedies, dramas, news programs, and action movies all competing for our attention. As it is, the radio and TV signals vary in vibration or frequency, so that each signal remains distinct even though they're all jumbled together in the same space. That way, the electronic circuits within a TV or radio can tune in to one signal, allowing us to hear only one program sent by only one station. The signals are separated from us and from each other by frequency, so they can't overwhelm us or get all mixed up with each other.

The room is also filled with countless subtle worlds beyond the physical world—all teeming with life. If our eyes and ears could see and hear those nonphysical realms, the room would be incomprehensibly crowded, and we would be completely overwhelmed by the sights and sounds of the many entities here among us. While the many worlds of spirit all inhabit the same space, each realm remains distinct by its vibration—again, like radio waves jumbled together in this room. In this case it is not a radio or TV frequency, but rather the vibration of consciousness that makes each realm of existence unique and discrete, so that the inhabitants and activities of that realm aren't disturbed by the many other beings inhabiting other realms, all teeming with life.

Some individuals are able to tune in with their minds to some of those other invisible worlds. Those who tune in to divine worlds of love and wisdom and receive impressions from ethereal beings are sometimes called *inspired* or *genius* or *spiritual masters*. Those who tune in to departed loved ones and wise beings and receive explicit messages from them are called *psychics, channels,* and *mediums.* Those who tune in to troubled beings stuck near the earth and receive malevolent messages and compulsions are called such names as *schizophrenic* and *psychopathic.* Spiritual interaction in our lives can result in experiences ranging from enlightenment to insanity. We shouldn't assume that only psychics, spiritualists, and schizophrenics can make contact with the spirit realms. We all tune in to some of those realms in our dreams, when the conscious, day-to-day mind switches off and the five physical senses close down for the night. Our finer senses, which transcend time and space, are activated when our physical body goes to sleep, and our spirit body ventures out to explore and experience those other realities. Those journeys provide the substance for most of our dreams, daydreams, and intuitive flashes.

We can also learn to tune in to some of those many realms through meditation, in which case we learn to adjust the vibration of our consciousness. Meditative states are like sleep states and dream states, except that we usually maintain some degree of conscious awareness. Our experiences in other realms don't get washed away like a dream when we return from a meditative state. There are technologies, such as the Monroe Institute's Hemi-Sync, that send alternating pulses of sound to the left and right hemispheres of the brain, moving it into the dream state or the sleep state to get our conscious mind in touch with other realms of existence. These technologies open mental communications with the spirit worlds, accomplishing in a matter of days, or even minutes, techniques of altering consciousness that would traditionally take spiritual adepts years to master.

Theoretically, if we had the right technologies, as well as psychospiritual readiness, we could tune in to the various realms with radio- and TV-like devices and indulge in interpersonal, interworld, high-tech communication. We could call Aunt Margaret on the phone, regardless of whether she lives in the next city or in the next world.

That theory is starting to become reality. We are learning what kinds of technologies it will take to get in touch with those other realms, and one thing we're learning is that there will have to be a marriage of mind and machine in ways that today are only dreamed of. That's what ITC is all about.

As you might imagine, before developing such subtle technologies, it is helpful first to understand the nature of the various realms and who inhabits them. It's not an easy task, since the various worlds of existence are virtually infinite in number and variety. As Jesus said, "My Father's house has many mansions." Through the centuries, different schools of esoteric thought and different religions have tried to classify the worlds of spirit in different ways. Hinduism, Judaism, Tibetan Buddhism, Christianity, Islam, and more modern institutions such as Theosophy, Eckankar, and the Monroe Institute all have their own systems of classifying the various worlds of spirit. We'll look at a very basic model or roadmap of the spirit worlds that some ITC researchers use today, because it is reasonably compatible with all the more elaborate models. That model provides a good springboard for exploring the richly diverse worlds of spirit.

There are many worlds of spirit, all superimposed over our physical world. Entities in those worlds sometimes interact with our world, and we attract into our lives spirits who resonate with our disposition. As a rule, if we're happy and loving, so are the spirits who are close to us and affect our lives. If we're generally fearful or grumpy, then the spirits involved in our life will probably stir up those troubled feelings even more. That's an oversimplification of what is sometimes called the *Law of Resonance,* but it gives you an idea. Essentially, birds of a feather flock together, even when those birds are living in different dimensions from each other.

Armed with spiritual understanding and various psychospiritual techniques, we can learn to control the types of spiritual influences upon our lives.

CHAPTER THREE

PICTURES FROM THE OTHER SIDE

The spirit worlds are right here, all around us, all jumbled together in the same space. This becomes strikingly clear in images I get with a Polaroid camera in the presence of the luminator. The invisible inhabitants of those worlds can become visible under the right conditions. They simply move into our personal space and superimpose their bodies over ours, in a way that seems strange to us in our world, but which is probably quite natural in their world, where time and space are illusory, and where beings are drawn to other beings of like disposition by the Law of Resonance.

The faces in these special Polaroid photographs are always superimposed, in part or in whole, over the human face. Apparently our spirit friends draw upon certain bodily substances of us humans in order to show themselves on film. That, I believe, is why the spirit faces are always superimposed over, never separate from and posing beside, the human face.

Sometimes the human face and spirit face are blended together as though the photo were a double exposure (see photos 11, Aaron, and 12, Andy). In the photo of Aaron (photo 11),

Aaron is the lower right face that's barely visible. The more prominent face above Aaron in that photo is an unidentified spirit, probably a member of my spirit group who was in my lab the evening I took this picture. (Everyone who gets involved in spirit communication gradually attracts a group of interested, supportive spirits around his or her work, and I'm sure that many faces that show up in my lab belong to those invisible friends of mine.)

Andy (photo 12) attended my seminar in Ohio in October 2002. As his photo developed, he felt the presence of his grandpa, Frank Trunzo, a kind-hearted, dapper man from southern Italy whose deep love of animals had rubbed off on Andy. There apparently is some soul connection between the two, as Andy has had several lucid dreams of his grandpa, in which he could feel Frank's stubble and smell the Brylcreem in his hair as they hugged. Andy recalls exclaiming, "Oh my God, Grandpa, you're alive." The face on the right could be Grandpa Frank, or it could be Andy's own astral body separating for a moment from the physical body. In any case, Andy was moved by the experience that evening and has since become a video ITC experimenter.

Sometimes the spirit face is looking off at a slight angle, offset from the human face (photo 13, Connie). This Pennsylvania woman (name changed by request) lost her son when he was only twenty-two years old, but the powerful heart connection remains, as evidenced in her picture, in which her late son poses at her throat chakra.

I've received swarthy spirit faces superimposed over light-skinned people (photo 14, Missy). Missy was photographed in Colorado Springs by Jack Stucki during my workshop at the Celebration Fair on April 19, 2002. That's Missy on the right, and the black fellow on the left resembles one of her husband's friends, who had died a few years earlier.

There have been male spirits superimposed over female subjects. Sometimes the male spirit face is offset from the

1. Gary (p. xii)

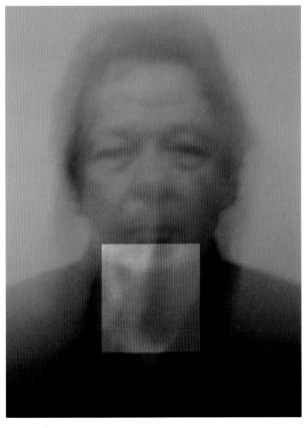

2. Gary (p. xii)

3. Mark (p. 5)

4. Mark (p. 5)

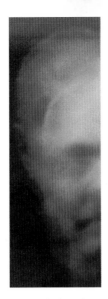 

5. Mark (p. 6)   6. Mark (p. 6)

7. Mark (p. 6)   8. Mark (p. 6)

9. Blair (p. 6)   10. Willis (p. 6)

11. Aaron (p. 11)

12. Andy (p. 11)

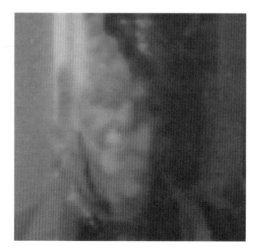

13. Connie (p. 12)

14. Missy (p 12)

15. Judith (p. 13)

16. Lisa (p. 13)

17. Meme (p. 13)

18. Meme (p. 13)

19. Meme (p. 13)

20. Meme (p. 13)

21. Mark (p. 13)

22. Blair (p. 13)

woman's face, and sometimes it takes over the woman's face completely. Judith (photo 15) participated in a workshop that Jack Stucki and I held in Kansas City, and a male spirit face showed up, with his eyes at the level of her mouth. Lisa (photo 16) attended my workshop in New York in 2004, and her face was completely replaced by a male face.

Sometimes two spirit faces appear and push the human face right out of the picture. Meme attended my workshop at the Edgar Cayce ARE Center in New York City on May 14, 2005. A sensitive woman, Meme often experiences spiritual intervention in her life. At home, she says, strange things happen on her computer, including text appearing on the screen when no one is physically present. In one message she received the words "Timestream" and "Juno," the names of two spirit groups known to be actively working on ITC projects. At the New York workshop we received one picture (photo 18, Meme) that had the faint image of a spirit in the stereotypical white, flowing gown. (Some people might argue that the gown is just a blur of Meme's white T-shirt caused by camera motion, but if you'll notice, Meme's face and the plants behind her are clearly in focus.)

Later on, Meme put on a pink sweater (photo 19), and she received a stunning photo of two distinct spirit faces (photo 20) replacing her own face. On the left is a nice-looking young man, and below and to the right is a wise-looking older woman. These are probably two of the guides who protect and support Meme and the ITC miracles that are starting to occur in her life.

Sometimes the face in the picture seems divided in two— human on the left, spirit on the right. One evening I was holding our cat Sebastian, hoping we might get a picture of our other cat Konrad, who had died the previous year. Instead, my father Blair Macy came through, appearing as he had looked as a young man (photo 21, Mark). Studying that picture of me, you can see that the right half of the face resembles my dad (photo 22, Blair). The other half-face in the photo is mine.

Sometimes the spirit face is in profile, with the nose of the spirit close to where the person's ear should be. This picture of me had a strange aberration on the right side of my face (photos 23 and 24, Mark). Upon closer examination, I realized it was my father again, peering out from the side of my head, in profile. This was Dad as he appeared in later life, bald. (Compare photo 24, Mark, with photo 9, Blair.) The image stirred a memory from my childhood. For many years Dad wrote a newspaper column called Behind the Eight-ball. Always at the top of that column was a small caricature of Dad peering out from behind a pool ball (photo 25, Blair). Knowing his sense of humor, I suspect there is a connection. He turned up in my photo, making me the eight-ball. Ha!

I've had lots of spirits posing with me over the years (photos 26–31). So have my wife and son (photos 32, Regina, to 37, Aaron). The two pairs of pictures of me (photos 26–29, Mark) were taken during weekly meetings of my research group between 1999 and 2001. In each case the first picture set (photos 26 and 28) shows me with few or no anomalies. The faces in the other photos (photos 27 and 29) belong to someone else entirely. My face was replaced by spirit faces. The first spirit face (photo 27) belongs to an unidentified fellow who completely took over my face. The other spirit (photos 29 and 30) bears a resemblance to George Meek, the father of ITC research and a good friend of mine. About two-thirds of that face poses side-by-side with about two-thirds of my own face, while the remaining portions of both faces are overlapped.

Another picture of me (photo 31, Mark) contains a spirit face at the lower right of my face. The spirit resembles an old Native American friend of mine, Gene Standingbear. He was an artist who painted scenes from his Lakota heritage, and he died in the 1970s.

In other pictures you can see Regina (photos 32–34) and spirit faces that showed up in two of them (photos 33, 34). The male face in one photo (photo 33), whose eyes are at the level of Regina's mouth, bears some resemblance to her father. The other photo (photo 34) has two faces that are unfamiliar to us, a woman on the left with eyes slanted in other-worldly fashion, and a swarthy man on the right.

In November 1999, shortly after acquiring the luminator, I took a series of three pictures of our son Aaron (photos 35–37, Aaron) who was thirteen at the time. When the photos developed, there were two spirit faces that completely took over his face (photos 36 and 37), but neither Aaron nor I recognized the faces.

When I laid the pictures on the kitchen counter, Regina glanced at them and gasped. "That's my dad!" she exclaimed. "Aaron, that's your grandfather, John Hoys."

Regina ran upstairs and returned a few minutes later with a black and white photo of herself and her dad at the New Jersey shore when Regina was just three years old (photo 38, Regina and her father).

John had died just a few weeks after I met Regina, and I never had the chance to meet him. Now, through ITC, Aaron and I both have the opportunity to get to know him. The fact that we live in different worlds is not an insurmountable obstacle to fostering a rapport, thanks to ITC.

CHAPTER FOUR

A LITTLE SPOOKY AT FIRST

The luminator images give us an unprecedented glimpse into the worlds of spirit, and since most of us have never looked into those worlds through our physical eyes, these pictures might seem strange at first, even a little spooky. That's a natural reaction whenever a new aspect of reality is suddenly opened up to us.

When the telescope was invented four centuries ago, men like Galileo looked up into the heavens and were stunned to see sunspots, moons around Jupiter, rings around Saturn, and pockmarks on the moon. Galileo's findings rocked the world. Nearly all scientists and religious leaders throughout Europe at the time regarded the heavens as God's perfect creation—a divine light show arranged for the pleasure of man on earth, around whom and around which everything else revolved. The telescope shattered that neat view of life, showing the universe as an imperfect and rather chaotic place in which the earth was little more than a grain of sand along an endless cosmic beach—a radical, upsetting notion four hundred years ago.

To accept that humbling view through Galileo's telescope, seventeenth-century science and religion would have had to completely disassemble their model of reality, then build a new one based on the radical facts brought to bear by the new instrument. Mankind and earth would have had to relinquish their position at the center of the universe to become minor players in a much larger reality.

But the bigger picture made most people feel mentally and emotionally unstable, so some of them ignored the new findings, while others attacked the researchers who presented them. The Spanish Inquisition was underway at the time, and inquisitors decreed, "God is perfect, and God's creation is perfect. Man is imperfect, and man's creations are imperfect. Why should we look through an imperfect creation like a telescope to view God's perfect creation? Wouldn't that corrupt God's creation?" They demanded that Galileo renounce his findings or face imprisonment or death. Galileo begrudgingly recanted his revolutionary cosmic view, at least publicly, even though he knew it was right.

The spirit faces in this book might be as disturbing to many modern scientists as the telescopic view of the universe was to seventeenth-century scientists. For science today, embracing the concept of the human spirit and afterlife is probably impossible without dismantling the current scientific paradigm and building a new one, using spirituality as the foundation. The new paradigm will probably go something like this: Many dimensions or levels of existence are superimposed over our physical universe; they're teeming with life, and they're all jumbled together in the same space, separated not by time or space but by vibration, like radio and TV signals in a room. In fact, time and space, as well as gravity, are illusions of the physical world—what Hindus call *maya* and what Buddhists call *samsara*. Beings in all of the various worlds are attracted to each other by the Law of Resonance.

These are the kinds of ideas that future science will embrace warmly; of that I have no doubt. Meanwhile, trying to convince today's mainstream scientists about spiritual reality is nearly impossible.

We each have our own personal vision of how the world works. We have a mental model of what reality is all about. Our personal model is formed by everything we've been taught in school and by our parents, the things we've read in the media and seen in movies, and the various situations and interactions that we experience in our day-to-day lives. All these impressions stream into our mind through the five senses to form this model of reality.

As new information comes in, our mind tries to accommodate it by adjusting the model. But if the information presents a danger to our model—if it contains information that won't fit unless we completely dismantle the model and build a new one—then our mind will usually reject that new information outright. It doesn't matter how obvious and rational the new information is. If it threatens the existing model, the mind becomes boggled and rejects it. That could be called the boggle point. Reaching the boggle point happens a lot in this world, and it's a major cause of closed-mindedness. So it's inevitable that some readers, especially many conventional scientists, will reject the information in this book outright because their minds have been boggled.

All of the images and messages included in this book are genuine; nothing has been contrived or faked. Photos in this book have been, in some cases, enlarged or highlighted to look clean and neat and to show details that would otherwise be hard to see. I've also cleared away extraneous smudges. The original pictures are either on file in my office or in the possession of the people who posed for the pictures. All of my explanations and descriptions of contacts with nonphysical beings are true and accurate, to the very best of my knowledge at the time of this writing. In particular, the spirit faces on Polaroid film provide proof of the afterlife—proof that would require intellectual gyrations to discount.

Historically, when science has been unable to fit new data into its existing paradigm, the result has been intellectual gyrations—the scientific version of fitting a square peg into a round hole. Around AD 100 Ptolemy and other Greek scientists believed that the earth was at the center of the universe. As centuries passed, astronomers charting the motion of heavenly bodies determined that if the earth was really at the center of the universe, then the sun and planets would have to be doing bizarre epicycles around it. That reasoning persisted until around 1500, when Copernicus showed that the earth revolved around the sun, not vice versa. Then all the astronomers' findings of the preceding centuries fell neatly into place.

Two hundred years later, around the time of Isaac Newton, science decided that everything could be explained through natural law, and spiritual existence was merely a myth. Again, centuries passed, and scientists began to encounter all sorts of weird claims that they couldn't easily explain. For example, they would hear very similar reports from different people who had died and been revived. Upon death these people reported going through a tunnel to a place of light, transcending space and time, and being immersed in peace, tranquility, and a oneness with all. Since these spiritual experiences didn't fit into the scientific paradigm, neuroscientists developed explanations involving the release of endorphins, reactions between the right and left superior parietal lobes, the mind-altering effects of anesthetic drugs, anoxia, hypercarbia, and temporal-lobe stimulation. Intellectual gyrations.

One day soon it will become apparent to mainstream science that the physical universe is just a small, illusory piece of God's much grander spiritual domain, and then all of the so-called phenomena and anomalies reported in recent centuries—angels, ghosts, near-death experiences, miracle healings, trance channeling, prophecies, and so on—will suddenly fall neatly into place.

Meanwhile there is a wide chasm between modern science and the human spirit. String theory and quantum physics are closing the gap with their focus on multiple dimensions and the creative power of consciousness (respectively). I would also bet that every scientist throughout history becomes convinced of spiritual existence sooner or later—if not before they die, then shortly afterwards. I'm sure many people are surprised to find that life goes on after they die, but they soon accept it. (Interestingly enough, we are told that some of the most skeptical people retain their skepticism once they've died. They accept spiritual existence, but no longer believe in life on earth; they think it was just a dream.)

There are many scientists on the other side who are fully aware of the truth. ITC researchers have known since the 1980s that teams of deceased scientists are working together to open communication channels with their counterparts on earth. I once received a voice through my radios that said, "Thomas A. to Winston," and I'm reasonably certain it was Thomas Alva Edison trying to get the attention of Winston Franklin, who began leading the Institute of Noetic Sciences after the death of Willis Harman. Colleagues of mine in Europe have received pictures and messages from Thomas Edison and other spirit beings with familiar names: Albert Einstein, Marie Curie, Konrad Lorenz, Henri Sainte-Claire de Ville, and Paracelsus, to name a few.

In March 2001 I received a picture that I believe is of Einstein (photos 40 and 41, Rich). He showed up over the face of Rich (photo 39), the scientific-technical member of my local research team from 1999 to 2001. Our spirit friends can change their appearance to look old or young, and very often they appear in a way that we on earth would easily recognize, perhaps resembling a familiar photograph taken during their lifetime. The spirit face in Rich's picture bore an uncanny resemblance to a famous public-domain photo of Einstein (photo 42, Albert).

One fellow told me that the faces in the photos can't possibly be spirits and the pictures must be faked. When I reminded him that the Polaroid photos could not have been manipulated in any way because of the nature of the Polaroid process, he then argued that the unusual faces are probably the result of double exposure or camera movement in a low-light situation. When I showed him a photo containing two faces, both of which are very clear and distinct (one male, one female), he suggested that maybe one face had been exposed to that print accidentally during the previous print's exposure. I said that as far as I knew, that's not possible with a Polaroid 600 camera. He thought for a moment, then got intrigued. He wondered if the thoughts, hopes, or expectations of the photographer or subject were somehow being impinged on the film. I asked him why the notion of human thoughts being captured on film is easier to believe than the idea of spirits being captured on film. He answered simply that they can't be spirit faces, because spirits don't exist.

That's an example of the boggle point at work and the intellectual gyrations that result. It's easier to weave complex, fanciful scenarios than to tear down one's belief system and to build a new one on a simple, new foundation—in this case, a foundation of spiritual reality. I myself have sometimes wondered if our thoughts and expectations can somehow manifest on film, but my experiences and results in ITC research have not yet confirmed that possibility, while they definitely have confirmed spiritual manifestation.

CHAPTER FIVE

ABOUT THOSE PICTURES AND THE LUMINATOR

When I got out of the navy in 1973, I drove across the Midwest in my new car with my new Colorado license plates to visit my brother and his family in New York. John Denver's new song "Rocky Mountain High" played on the car radio several times during the trip, and each time it felt like my car was floating as I sang along. Denver's music has resonated with me ever since. So it wasn't a surprise when Denver's image appeared in a photo during my seminar nearly thirty years later—five years after the singer had died in a plane crash in 1997.

I was invited to share my ITC research at the Celebration Metaphysical Fair on April 20, 2002, in Colorado Springs. It was a good opportunity for something miraculous to happen because there would be two luminators present.

Jack Stucki (photo 43, Jack and his luminator) is a Colorado Springs therapist who uses his luminator in his practice. In fact, it was the spirit faces caught on Polaroid film in Jack's therapy sessions with clients that first grabbed my attention and compelled me to acquire a luminator for my own use back in 1999. Jack and I get some of our best results when we pool our resources. With both luminators running, we sometimes get pictures with strikingly clear spirit faces. He joined me during the workshop, and we put both luminators on stage, creating a powerful field of subtle energy. We took pictures of all the participants, and several remarkable pictures emerged. The most amazing was one of John Denver (photos 44–45, Joy). For months I had been corresponding with friends of the late singer, and we hoped he would make contact with us. One particular acquaintance of Denver's met with Jack and me in the weeks leading up to the workshop, and she attended our workshop session. I believe that her presence, as well as my own appreciation for Denver and his music, helped attract his spirit to our event that day. I was naturally pleased—delighted, actually—to know that the famous singer was interested in ITC.

At first I was surprised that Denver did not appear in the picture of his acquaintance, but appeared instead in a picture of Joy Schilling, owner of a metaphysical bookstore in Colorado Springs; she had never met the singer. However, it occurred to me that Joy seems to have an inner light and charisma that also glowed in Denver, leading me to suspect that there is a spiritual resonance between the two. That resonant condition seems to be more important than lifetime familiarity in determining who will visit whom when people in spirit come close to our world to make contact.

Most of the work involved in making these pictures is done on our spirits friends' side. They have to move close to our world in vibration and synchronize with our time and space. The main things we provide from this side are low-lighting conditions and the basic Polaroid photo process—that is, a Polaroid 600 camera and lots and lots of film. We take all of our pictures in normal indoor lighting: incandescent, fluorescent, or a combination of the two. Sunlight, halogen lighting, and other light sources have not been as effective. In fact, direct sunlight washes away all spirit effects. To achieve the low-lighting conditions, we cover the camera's flash unit with a strip of black electrician's tape, then cut a small, sesame seed-sized hole in the tape to allow just a flicker of light during each exposure.

The luminator was developed by Michigan inventor Patrick Richards. It has two counter-rotating fans that pull air into vents at the base of the unit and blow it out through the vents at the top. The air passes through a Plexiglas barrel lined with liquid-filled rings. The liquid is water based. Beyond that I know little about the physics of the luminator, but I can speculate. Meta-physicians have long known that water acts as a crystal—storing consciousness in the form of vibrations, as a battery stores electricity—and that might be the working principle behind the luminator. Apparently the water in each ring has been programmed—maybe psychospiritually—with certain frequencies and intentions. According to legend, great human civilizations of the distant past used crystals to wield tremendous power and energy, and it seems that some modern inventors, such as Patrick Richards, are once again learning techniques to tap the vast power of subtle energies.

Subtle energies are those imperceptible vibrations of conscious life that exist outside the electromagnetic spectrum—beyond the scope of modern scientific understanding. Subtle energies are not really subtle at all. They only seem subtle as they brush up against our dense and heavy world, but in their own dimensions they embody the vast power of creation itself.

As we learn to put these subtle energies to work here on earth, my research suggests that we will inherit power far beyond what we today can even imagine—unlimited, nonpolluting energy as envisioned by Nikola Tesla. We'll also achieve direct access to other dimensions of existence, as seen in the luminator images and in the broader field of ITC.

One obstacle to the mastery of subtle energy in our world is education. When most people on earth can understand the power of consciousness and subtle-energy technologies the way we understand the reality of nuclear energy, then perhaps these new technologies will begin to transform the world.

I believe that the luminator establishes a field of subtle energy that melts away the boundary between the physical world and rather dense spiritual worlds that are close by in vibration. It allows people in spirit to come unusually close to us and draw upon our bodily substances (what spiritualists call *ectoplasm*), so that the spirit people can become a little bit denser than usual—dense enough to show up on Polaroid film—but still remain just out of the range of normal human vision. As the two realms overlap, a blurriness can result in the pictures. Sometimes it looks like a double exposure; we can see the physical objects and their spirit-world counterparts, which exist in a superimposed world of slightly finer vibration.

There are nine luminators in the world at the time of this writing, and eight of them are in the possession of therapists. Mine is the only luminator used primarily for a nontherapeutic purpose—ITC. The other eight are used for healing purposes—for example, as an alternative to muscle testing and pendulum testing.

In muscle testing, or applied kinesiology, a client might hold a bottle of medicine in one hand, close to the chest, while extending the other arm out. The therapist will pull down on the outstretched arm to determine if the medicine is helpful or harmful for a client. Strong resistance indicates good medicine, but if the arm seems weak, the medicine will weaken the client.

A pendulum is frequently used for similar purposes. The pendulum, often a crystal on a string or chain, is held over the client or whatever is being tested, and its behavior indicates a positive or negative condition. For example, the pendulum spinning in a circle might indicate yes, while swinging back and forth might indicate no.

Some people wonder if muscle-testing and pendulum techniques are too subjective. The therapist could unconsciously (or consciously) exert greater or lesser force on the client's arm, or cause the pendulum to circle or swing. I know by experience that kinesiology and pendulums can be effective and accurate clinical techniques, but I suspect they are also inaccurate and too subjective at times.

The luminator provides a more objective technique to do such testing. Photos of clients can come out clear, indicating a positive condition and a coherence of body, mind, and spirit; or the photos can be extremely blurry, as though the client is lost in a mist, which indicates a negative, incoherent condition. Either result can occur while the camera is being held perfectly still. Jack and presumably other therapists with luminators regard the faces as spirits who are having helpful or harmful influences on the client. In matters of spirit, intention plays an important role in the results. If the owner of a luminator is a therapist who wants blurry images to indicate unhealthy conditions and clear images to indicate healthy conditions, then those are the results that will evolve with the help of his spiritual healing team—the spirit beings who work with that therapist in his treatment of clients. If, on the other hand, the owner of a luminator is like me—an ITC researcher who wants faces of loved ones, spirit guides, members of my spirit team, and other invisibles to show up on film—then those results will evolve in our work. That is the nature of subtle energy technologies.

The luminator could be useful in many professions, including mental-health care, medicine, and criminal law. It's all a matter of intention. What exactly do we want to see as the result of our work with subtle energy technologies and techniques?

For centuries, mystics and sages have asked that question of people who come to them for wisdom and answers to life's mysteries: They ask the seeker, "What is it you want? What do you *really* want?"

When a person can answer that question with certainty and resolve, invisible forces mobilize to bring those desires to fruition. That is the simple truth behind every spiritual practice ranging from prayer to miracle healings. It is also one of the most fundamental facts of day-to-day life; we create our reality with focused desire and intention. Whenever we humans are passionate about something, there are always invisible forces (spiritual beings) at work, bringing the object of our passions to bear—for better or worse, depending on the nature of our passions.

In the case of the luminator images, some of those invisible forces become visible. Those forces are our spirit guides, our departed loved ones, and in my case, my invisible team of spirit collaborators.

CHAPTER SIX

THE MIRACLE OF ITC RESEARCH

My spirit encounters are not limited to pictures. I've been involved in the young field of ITC research since 1992, using technologies to contact the other side, and as a result I've had numerous spiritual experiences that were mind boggling and soul stirring. On one occasion I spoke on the phone for nearly fifteen minutes with a departed colleague named Konstantin Raudive, a Latvian psychologist who had been a pioneer in spirit communication before he died. We discussed my equipment, my colleagues, and various other topics. He told me that my colleagues and I were being monitored on computer-like terminals on the other side. They saw us as a collection of points on a screen, all connected by lines indicating collaboration and friendship. There were a few large points representing key members, and only from those major points could new lines be drawn.

That phone call was one of the most miraculous experiences of my life so far. For the first minute or so I was nervous, even though at the time it should have been a rather matter-of-fact experience because of the research I was involved in and also because it was not my first spirit phone call. I had enjoyed several shorter other-worldly phone calls before that one. Still, the very thought of chatting on the phone with the other side is quite extraordinary.

Someday I believe phone calls across the veil will be as commonplace as phone calls across the Atlantic, but for now they are extremely rare, even for ITC researchers. It's more common nowadays, in the opening years of the twenty-first century, for me to find tiny voices on tape while playing back recorded chats and phone calls with people on earth. Neither I nor the persons I'm chatting with can hear the spirit voices during our conversations, but when playing back the tape, the voices are clearly present. On one occasion I was talking to an attorney by phone about possible troubles ITC researchers might have trying to copyright our contacts. The lawyer was saying, "So it's kind of a catch-22. I mean I don't know how you say it's an original work of authorship. . . ."

When the attorney paused to collect his thoughts, the spirit's angry voice broke in, "Not when somebody . . ."

But the end of the spirit's message was washed out and lost when the attorney continued, ". . . if in fact you're claiming that it was authored by someone else. . . ."

That surprise contact came at a time of troubles among ITC researchers living in different countries. There were jealousies, false accusations, and angry reactions that destroyed several years of friendship and collaboration, a subject of my previous book, *Miracles in the Storm*. We've found that the moods and dispositions of our spirit communicators often reflect our own. When we're happy, we're working with happy spirits. When we're afraid or resentful, we find ourselves working with spirits who stir up those troubled feelings even more. I'm learning that this Law of Resonance is true for everyone, not just ITC researchers.

On another occasion, while my wife Regina and I were visiting my mom on February 2, 2005, to discuss her will and trust, I brought a tape recorder along to get all the details on tape, and a friendly spirit voice broke in very clearly on tape, saying, "Hello, Mark. Ed Bingham." The three of us weren't aware of the presence of this Ed Bingham fellow that day, but he was obviously there with us in Mom's kitchen. Again, the voice was inaudible until I played back the tape, and then it was loud and clear.

The name Bingham is associated with one of my spirit friends, a nineteenth-century Brooklyn journalist named Arthur Beckwith, who died the same night the Titanic sank. Arthur told us about himself in a detailed computer contact in Luxembourg on October 7, 1995. Further research indicated that he had lived on Schermerhorn Street in the boarding house of a Canadian carpet salesman named J. A. Bingham, and Beckwith's son Arthur Jr. had married one of Bingham's stepdaughters. So I do have a connection to a family of Binghams. But who exactly is Ed Bingham, and is there a connection? I haven't the foggiest idea at this time. Small mysteries such as this (as well as the names behind most of the faces that appear in our luminator photos) sometimes get answered in the course of this work, so patience is a virtue in ITC research.

I suspect that I share a spiritual resonance with Arthur Beckwith, who is now working with my ITC spirit group. I graduated from college in 1977 with a degree in journalism, and my father and grandfather both had been journalists. That seems to be how a spirit group gradually develops around an ITC researcher. As he or she becomes more aware of the spirit worlds, his or her interests are tuned in to by compatible spirits—spirits who resonate with the experimenter's disposition, interests, and intentions—and a bridge is slowly built across dimensions.

On one occasion Beckwith himself broke through my short-wave radio sound,[2] saying clearly, "Time just passes here." I wasn't sure at the time whose voice it was, but the next day colleagues of mine in Europe received a computer contact confirming that it was the voice of Beckwith.

On another occasion, five of us got together in the Luxembourg flat of Maggy Harsch-Fischbach in the summer of 1994, and the deep voice of our spirit friend Konstantin Raudive broke through the radio sounds, saying in his northern European accent, "It can only work when the vibrations of those present are in complete harmony, and when their aims and intentions are pure." He went on to convey a meaningful personal message to each person present. He told me, "Last but not least, Mark Macy. You know by experience, Mark, how dangerous drugs of all kinds can be. Try to warn humanity that they not only alter their present lives on your side, but also influence in a negative way their future lives. Go on with your experiences, and you will see that the bridge to the States will soon be strengthened. Regina, as your twin soul, can help you a lot. Listen to her inner voice, and you will be in the right way."

That's typical of many ITC contacts; our spirit friends tend to pack a lot of information into short messages. Konstantin's opening statement tells us that the researchers working together on an ITC project not only have to follow the same game plan, so to speak, but they also can't be driven by envy or greed or fear or other emotions that ruin the purity of our intentions. Furthermore, our vibrations (the essence of our consciousness) have to be in harmony; we have to be resonant. A large article—maybe an entire book—could be devoted to that opening line.

---

[2] Like many other ITC experimenters, I use radios in some of my experiments to contact the other side. Sometimes I feel a compulsion to turn on the radios to experiment at a particular time of day. Other experimenters sometimes hear a voice in their head recommending a particular time and maybe radio frequency as well. In a few cases experimenters have even received phone calls or computer contacts from spirit friends providing details of when and how they should prepare for a contact attempt through radio or TV.

As far as his personal message to me, Konstantin tapped into aspects of my personality, my goals, my fears, and my tendencies that I have always tried to keep private and secret. He was suggesting in a very subtle and tactful way that secrecy can cause problems for people working together on a spiritual project such as ITC.

Konstantin mentioned drugs. I smoked a bit of marijuana in my twenties. I experimented with other recreational drugs just a few times before I felt control of my life slipping away, so I quit. I was more vulnerable to the more acceptable drugs—buying whiskey, rum, and gin by the half-gallon, drinking pots of coffee and tea while writing, and smoking two or three packs of cigarettes a day—until I realized they were the most dangerous of all for me, because of their social acceptability. I didn't know I was addicted until it was too late. When I had to quit smoking, I took up chewing tobacco. It satisfied my nicotine craving, so I overlooked the fact that it was a messy, unhealthy habit.

After my bout with colon cancer in 1988, my body was super sensitive, and indulging in those habits would nearly send me into convulsions. To this day I am still sensitive to those things I'd overindulged in, so I avoid them as a rule. I still have a proclivity to drugs, though. I grew fond of the prescription painkillers and the mellow glow I felt in the hospital after the surgery, so I kept using them as long as I could in the ensuing months.

I remember on one occasion in 1992, shortly after getting involved in ITC, I was in North Carolina visiting George Meek, the father of ITC research. He had very quickly become my close friend and guru, helping me to get immersed in spirituality. As I sat in his kitchen, talking to him and his housekeeper, Loree, I noticed a bottle of Percocet. Later on, when I was alone in the kitchen, I took a pill from the bottle and put it in my pocket to enjoy that evening.

As soon as I heard Konstantin's voice on the radio two years later in Europe, I recalled that moment, and I almost felt a subtle thump on the side of the head by the collective finger of our spirit group. I could almost hear some of them (especially George's departed wife, Jeannette) asking me, "What were you *thinking?*"

We all make bad choices from time to time. We're only human, after all. But some choices are worse than others. Konstantin's warning about drug addiction is especially important for people today.

I've always wanted to address the world and help humanity solve its problems, even before I had anything useful to share. I went through the grueling process of getting educated, in part by pursuing college degrees and military electronics training, and in part by reading most of a one-volume encyclopedia while I lived alone. In the years leading up to my cancer, I contacted leading thinkers from around the world and published several books about world affairs—books filled with new ideas about economics, political systems, religions, social systems, biological systems, and more, all of which I still believe are quite revolutionary and hold great promise.

For example, what would it take to prevent strong nations that crave oil from bullying weaker nations that are rich in oil? An oil-reliant nation is like a heroin addict, always craving more for a quick fix, even though the more it uses, the sicker it becomes—the classic definition of addiction. The right and decent action of any addict is inner work to overcome its desperate reliance. The wrong action is to steal—knocking over a liquor store for money to buy drugs or unleashing a high-tech Armageddon on a Third World country in order to seize control of its economy and resources.[3] That's just one example of the information I was gathering to satisfy my urge to warn humanity.

Once I became immersed in spirituality, those potentially earth-shaking notions lost a lot of their punch for me. I sud-

[3] That particular analogy was shared with me by Dr. Paul Wachtel, author of *The Poverty of Affluence* (Gabriola Island, BC: New Society Publishers, 1989).

denly saw that spiritual forces have a bigger impact on the affairs of earth and mankind than people realize—maybe more than any of the more grounded disciplines traditionally equated with world affairs. But through it all I still have this strong compulsion to warn humanity. Konstantin Raudive and the spirit group obviously know that I'd be motivated by that message, because, as far as I know, no other ITC researcher was ever told to warn humanity about anything.

And finally, there were Konstantin's comments about Regina. She and I met when we were in our mid-thirties. She'd been through some difficult times and learned a lot about nutrition, spirituality, and human relationships, whereas I hadn't a clue about any of those things and didn't really care. She tried to get me to eat whole grains and fresh fruits and vegetables, but I refused to give up my diet of meat and grease. She told me how important it is for people, especially for men, to get in touch with their emotions and to share their feelings, and my eyes rolled by reflex as stoic images of John Wayne and Charles Bronson flashed through my head.

I'm sure that my stubbornness on all of these issues was like Miracle-Gro for the tumor in my colon. The cancer hit hard, and it began to dawn on me as I healed that Regina had been right about most of these things. Konstantin and our spirit friends wanted to make that point clear to me. If you think that his comment, "Listen to her inner voice and you will be in the right way," gave her extra power in the marriage, you're right—and that's a good thing.

All that information was packed into that short radio contact. A year later, in 1995, Maggy Harsch-Fischbach and I; her husband, Jules Harsch; my friends Juliette Hollister and Alison van Dyk, and nearly a dozen other scientists and researchers from eight countries founded a research panel called the International Network for Instrumental Transcommunication (INIT) at Dartington, England. We began to receive the most miraculous contacts imaginable, especially through computers in Europe. These are the true miracles of ITC research and the reason I do the work I do. The following five contacts were received via computer by experimenters in Luxembourg.

An ancient Chinese physician who lived in the city of Yo Lang 1,800 years ago now lives near the Hills of the Yellow Jade, a Chinese community in the spirit worlds. In a contact on January 23, 1996, he recalled that during his life on earth he met people who claimed to have certain powers to heal and to communicate with the dead, and he investigated those claims on behalf of the emperor. He found:

- Charlatans with no real mediumistic or healing skills who were lying to the people;
- Psychics and healers called *Wu*, who were honest and skilled, but their bizarre, crude methods corrupted China's proud esoteric heritage;
- Would-be spiritual masters whose laziness and superstitions attracted negative spirits into their own lives and into the lives of the peasants who took their words to heart;
- A few skilled practitioners whose humility, wisdom, and decency have survived the ages despite a rough road of insults and accusations during their lifetimes.

An African tribesman who was an experienced mountaineer and scout was killed and eaten by a lion many years ago. According to a message received on March 8, 1996, from our spirit colleagues, the tribesman M'Banga today serves as a guide when members of our spirit group take exploratory journeys through their world. On one recent expedition into the mountains they entered a cave and followed a faint violet beam of light into a large cavern, where diffused light glittered from the ceiling. A brilliant being was sitting in the center of the cavern, levitating a few inches off the ground. His face was morphing through many human faces—black, white, Asian, male, female, child, adult—until he shared words of wisdom with the visitors. He said that two types of spirits in particular can intervene directly into human affairs on earth:

- Those in spirit who are not too far removed from the earth in terms of attitudes and spiritual development (they move in and out of the lives of people on earth routinely), and
- Departed friends and loved ones who share a heart connection with people still on earth (although far removed from the affairs of earth, they have direct access to their loved ones here).

Other beings in the spirit worlds have little access to earthly ITC systems. In my research I've found two exceptions:

1. Deceased humans who have moved on to finer realms of spirit, but who choose to work in an ITC spirit group in order to help specific researchers on earth (they can "commute to work" to be close to us in vibration),
2. Ethereal beings who have special missions involving ITC (they seem to have few limitations).

An Arab spice dealer lived in Haybar during the time of the Prophet Muhammad (570–632), whom he had heard speak to the crowds on two occasions. In a contact received on June 27, 1996, the spice dealer recalled that after his death, the only person he had missed was his daughter-in-law, Fatima, who had taken care of him when he was old and gray.

Around the year 1400 (earth time) he was reunited with Fatima. They were both lonely and loved each other, so they've been together for six centuries in a bustling Arabian community called Yatrib Quastar, where he oversees the activities at the bazaar in his role as facilitator of the barter exchange system. (There is no money in the spirit worlds.) The bazaar is always buzzing with activity. Noisy dialogs flow in Aramaic, Greek, Arabic, and Persian as people trade bright clothes, balls of silk thread, and colorful tapestries. Camels haul goods from faraway lands while fragrances of spices and flowers fill the air. A typical day in paradise.

A Native American village thrived long ago on a big island at a time when rumors were spreading among Native American communities of strange men coming from across the water carrying deadly "thunder sticks." According to a message received on November 28, 1996, that village still thrives in the worlds of spirit. One elder typically wears a red-stained buckskin shirt with burned-in Native American symbols, along with a white fur cap. His house stands next to the medicine tipi along a river lined with poplar trees, not far from a stockade where gardens of corn and beans merge with an endless prairie of grass, waving like a rich, green ocean in the gentle spirit-world breezes. The villagers lead peaceful, contented lives in paradise. Their only annoyances have to do with missionaries of the Church of the Second Hope, a zealous spirit-world religious group of men and women who visit frequently and try to convert the villagers to their beliefs.

Through ITC systems, the elder tells us that his people feel that their bounteous spirit-world land is for everyone, and many white people are their friends. They honor and respect the Great Spirit, love each other, and never argue about religion, so they can't understand why these missionaries keep intruding, telling the community that their church's beliefs are right, the community's beliefs are wrong, and the people must change their beliefs.

Very recently, the village left to move among communities of Wanapum, Duwamish, Irokes, Yakima, Sauk Fox, Winnebagos, Choktaw, Lakota, and Flatheads, in a place where there are endless fields of grass, good rivers, and no religious zealots.

A Polynesian girl lives on a spirit-world island called Motu Toopua, which has coconut palms and pourau trees, hibiscus and tiare blossoms, much like the island she remembers more than a thousand years ago on earth. In a contact on April 18, 1995, she said she was recently sitting contentedly in the bay of her paradise village when the quiet evening was broken by familiar sounds of a tunnel opening—a sort of whooshing and gurgling, followed by a sound like surf breaking on rocks. A hole as large as a coconut opened in the air in front of her and quickly grew to the size of a large wooden cask. It pulsed in shades of deep blue, aquamarine, and turquoise. The twilight lit up into bright daylight as one of the Rainbow People—a term used for highly advanced spiritual beings who visit the paradise world of our ancestors on occasion—stepped through into the island girl's paradise world carrying an old woman, weak and frail, the wife of an ITC researcher in Europe. She had just died, and the great being urged the island people to nurse the woman back to health and youth.

The entire tribe liked the woman, and the woman enjoyed the activities of the village, especially the getting-in-touch rituals, in which the tribe members peer into our earth world through smoke that has been generated by burning special dried plants.

The visitor quickly regained her health among the island people, then embarked on a sailing ship to be reunited with family members elsewhere in the worlds of spirit.

As we can see from these five contacts, ITC is a project intended to encompass all mankind—not just one group or culture and certainly not just one researcher. ITC has to be a global venture in order for the ethereal beings to be involved at this point in mankind's development. One particular group of ethereal beings, The Seven, offers protection and guidance to the ITC project.

The vast complexity of the spirit worlds, from strange faces on Polaroid film, to detailed computer reports of life on the other side, to ethereal beings who glow in rainbow colors, sit in caves, and walk through invisible doorways into other worlds. How can we reconcile this mind-boggling information in our brains? That's what we'll try to do in part two.

PART TWO

A DEEPER LOOK INTO THE WORLDS OF SPIRIT

The next few chapters contain theories and a story of a journey through the spirit worlds, all based on factual information I have encountered in my research. I decided that along with the basic theories, a compelling story would be the best way to convey a subject as complex as the eternal, omnipresent worlds of spirit.

The experiences woven into this spirit world adventure are closely based on actual accounts that came from the other side either directly through ITC systems or through the minds of gifted mediums. The ITC information came through the systems of Maggy Harsch-Fischbach of Luxembourg and Adolf Homes of Germany, two of the most prolific ITC researchers in the 1990s. The ITC contacts were documented in the journals *Contact!* (which I published while I was in close collaboration with Mrs. Harsch-Fischbach) and *Transcommunication* (published by Prof. Dr. Ernst Senkowski, founder of Germany's Institute for Psychobiophysics and a close collaborator of Mr. Homes). The channeled material is from three books that I found to be accurate in their portrayal of the afterlife. I carefully selected the three books from different parts of the world because they show that the human spirit worlds are remarkably similar, despite cultural and geographic differences here on Earth:

From England: *Life in the World Unseen* (Two World Publishing, London: 1954), by Anthony Borgia, a gifted medium who channeled the thoughts of Hugh Benson, son of Edward Benson, Archbishop of Canterbury. Sensitive, artistic, and mystical, Hugh had become a priest and had written several books, including *The Necromancers* which, although popular, gave an unrealistic view of the spirit worlds, which Hugh had sorely regretted after his death in 1914 at age 43. Ethereal beings granted him a wish to correct his errors by delivering truth about the afterlife through a reliable source on earth, and Mr. Borgia was selected as that source.

From Brazil: *Nosso Lar: Our Spiritual Home* (first published by the Brazilian Spiritualistic Federation, Rio de Janeiro, 1944), by Francisco Xavier, another gifted medium and a prolific author. Xavier channeled the experiences of André Luis (Andy), an agnostic Brazilian Doctor who, dying in the 1930s, had been stunned to find a richer life awaiting him in paradise. After being educated by ethereal beings who showed him all facets of the spirit worlds, Andy was allowed to share his knowledge with humanity, through Xavier's honed mediumistic skills. As the book spread widely through the Portuguese-speaking world, American Salim Haddad took great pains to translate the book into English in a way that preserved the poetic, soul-stirring nature of the original text.

From India: *The Laws of The Spirit World* (1985), by Mrs. Khorshed R. Bhavnagri, whose sons Vispi, 30, and Ratoo, 29, died in a car accident in February, 1980. Devastated, their parents Rumi and Khorshed received solace from séances, where they learned that their sons had an important mission under the guidance of ethereal beings. A month after their death they began to communicate mentally with their mom, who took copious notes about the wondrous worlds of spirit where Vispi and Ratoo were now flourishing, and those notes became the substance of three books.

23. Mark (p. 14)

24. Mark (p. 14)

25. Blair (p.14)

26. Mark (p. 14)

27. Mark (p. 14)

28. Mark (p. 14)

29. Mark (p. 14)

30. Mark (p. 14)

31. Mark (p. 14)

32. Regina (p. 14)

33. Regina (p. 15)

34. Regina (p. 15)

35. Aaron (p. 15)

36. Aaron (p. 15)

37. Aaron (p. 15)　　　　　　38. Regina and her father (p. 15)

39. Rich (p. 21)

40. Rich (p. 21)

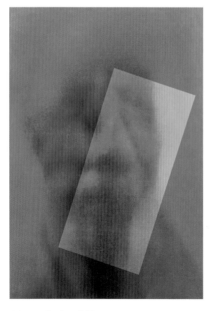

41. Rich (p. 21)

42. Albert (p. 21)

43. Jack and his luminator (p. 23)

44. Joy (p. 24)

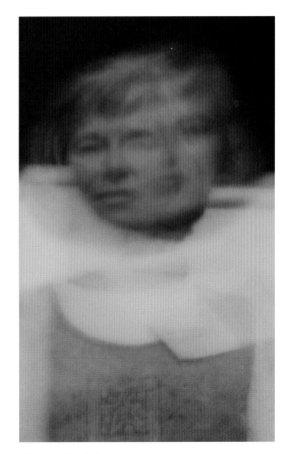

45. Joy (p. 24)

46. Tianna (p. 89)

47. Tianna (p. 93)

48. Tianna (p. 93)

49. William (p. 89)

CHAPTER SEVEN

⌗

THE WORLDS OF SPIRIT

When those invisible people come to pose in our photos in the presence of the luminator, or to talk to us on the phone, or plant images in our computer, where do they come from? Do dead people just hang around our world caught up in our affairs? Is the purpose of their lives to be engrossed in ours?

That's the way many of us seem to feel about the spirit worlds; we think of ghosts inhabiting our houses to scare us and angels manifesting miracles in our lives to help us out, as though everything in God's creation revolves around us and our world. The fact is, life is much more complex and far reaching than the affairs of earth, which are almost inconsequential in the larger scheme of things. Despite the complexity of the spirit worlds, we can boil down the concept of spiritual existence into a simple but useful model.

Through the centuries, human beings have studied and classified the spirit worlds in many ways. I have explored many of those systems of study, and my colleagues and I have actually talked directly with beings in various worlds through technologies. The classification system we developed from that research is accurate, as well as exceptionally comprehensive and appropriate for humans in today's world. If God, Shiva, the Archangel

Michael, a little gray extraterrestrial, or dear, departed Aunt Jane were to classify the various worlds of spirit from their perspectives, the classification system might be very different.

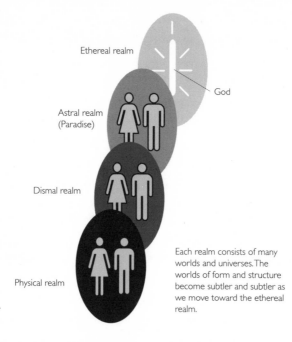

Ethereal realm

God

Astral realm
(Paradise)

Dismal realm

Physical realm

Each realm consists of many worlds and universes. The worlds of form and structure become subtler and subtler as we move toward the ethereal realm.

This model is especially suited to human beings in physical bodies on earth. Why? Because we are totally immersed, consciously, in an illusory world of forms and structures. This model divides reality into worlds of form and structure and the finer worlds beyond form and structure—worlds of pure consciousness (ethereal worlds). I subdivide the worlds of form and structure into three parts to represent (1) where we are now, the physical realm, (2) where some people get stuck after they die, the dismal realm, and (3) where most of us *should* go after we die, the astral realm.

The physical realm is composed of comparatively dense, slowly vibrating matter and energies. Our own vast physical universe, with its many stars and galaxies, is just one of many physical universes existing in parallel (or rather, superimposed over each other), separated from each other not by time or space, but by vibration, or frequency.

The dismal realm is a troubled place composed largely of the fears, doubts, and animosities that spin off the earth into subtler realms of existence. If you took the worst qualities of mankind and rolled them up into a dark, wretched world, you'd have the lowest reaches of the dismal realm. At the highest reaches of the dismal realm you find people much like us. Patterns of earthly thought and behavior are deeply etched, so these folks look much as they had looked on earth. As we move deeper into the dismal realm, its residents become more decrepit, blemished, and unhappy.

The astral realm is a place of form and structure much like our own physical world, though it is cleaner and purer, and the structures and activities in the astral realm are more malleable—adapting more smoothly to the thoughts and intentions of the astral residents, who include most people who once had lived here on earth. This is particularly true in the finer regions of the astral realm, where people live in astral bodies that are at the prime of life—age twenty-five to thirty-five in appearance—with no blemishes, facial hair, or deformities. They have overcome most of the patterns of troubled earthly thought—the fears and animosities—but they are still worldly in many ways. If you took all the best qualities of mankind and rolled them up into a paradise world, you would have the higher reaches of the astral realm—what Christians call heaven, what Muslims call Jannah, what Hindus call Pitraloka, and what Spiritualists call the Summerland. There are many worlds in the astral realm, and at its lowest reaches you find people much like us—people with facial hair, blemishes, obesity, cellulite, and other flaws of the physical world. This is the arbitrary point where the astral and dismal realms converge.

I and some of my ITC colleagues work with teams of men and women in the astral realm. They commute to work, in a sense, in order to show up in the luminator photos and to work with our equipment. They lower their vibration so that their spirit bodies become dense enough to move into astral regions close to the earth and to show up in this special photographic process.

As they move closer to our world, earthly patterns of body and mind begin to return.

The ethereal realm is a formless world consisting of the pure consciousness of its ethereal inhabitants, who exchange information faster and more efficiently than the supercomputers of our world. Ethereal beings possess the power to create entire worlds. If you took the perfect consciousness of the Christ, the Buddha, Mohammed, and the other great spiritual masters and multiplied it by a million, you might have a taste of the ethereal realm. Ethereal beings are of such a fine and subtle vibration that, to my knowledge, they do not show up in any luminator photos, at least not yet. As subtle technologies on earth improve, this could change.

God, or the Source, is at the center of all these realms. In fact, it is the pure non-vibrating light emitted by God that manifests as everything in every realm of existence. As this light—this perfect consciousness—leaves the Source, it starts to vibrate. It vibrates more and more slowly as it becomes further removed (in vibration, not distance) from the Source. That vibrating light then manifests as all of the countless worlds and spiritual communities and universes in the four realms.

Within each realm are many, many worlds and universes. All of these realms and the countless worlds within them exist in the same space, and they remain separate and distinct by the vibration or frequency of consciousness that forms each.

Our common soul purpose is one of the reasons I believe we physical human beings choose lifetimes on earth. There's a personal mission that we hope to achieve, and that's a subject of the last chapter. But I believe there's also a common soul purpose that we all share.

Our true self, our soul, is a piece of God, and it's located in the center of our being—a sort of eternal flame of perfect love and knowledge. Our common purpose, in my view, is to connect our conscious mind to that God self through such practices as prayer and meditation, and then to bring God's love and light into this world through our everyday thoughts, words, and actions.

In time and space, God is right here with us and also inside us. But in the physical realm we are *vibrationally* far removed from God, the source of love. God's love becomes dim here, and so pockets of chaos develop, which some cultures have labeled evil. Bringing more of God's love into this vibrational outpost means getting our conscious minds in touch with our souls, which are a part of the Source, pulling love from the Source through our soul and our mind, and releasing it out into the world through our thoughts, words, and actions. Reconnecting with our soul is our common purpose, the key to a future of peace, prosperity, and happiness on earth.

It's not an easy task for most of us. Our conscious mind begins to function at a very young age, and as information streams into our five senses, we become totally absorbed in the material world. Unless we are frequently reminded of our rich spiritual roots by our parents and community, most of us lose touch with our spiritual identity when we are just a few years old. It's too easy to get distracted by earthly things and to let our spiritual purpose fall by the wayside. It's easy to become distracted by the illusions of the physical world and to veer off the path of love into the chaotic pockets of negativity or evil.

Getting in touch with our soul is difficult for another reason, too. There are disruptive and harmful spiritual influences in the dismal realm. By stirring up hatred, fear, guilt, envy, and other troubled feelings within us, those dark forces can prevent us from getting in touch with our finer spiritual self.

A CAKE ANALOGY

Think of humanity and the physical realm as a child who has just turned seven. His mother is God, and his birthday cake represents the worlds of spirit.

The body of the cake would be the spiritual realms of form and structure—the dismal and astral realms. The decorative frosting would be the highest or subtlest worlds within the astral realm, sometimes called the Summerland—the sweetest, most colorful, most beautiful part of the cake. The bright, sparkling candles are angels and light beings whose warm collective glow forms the ethereal realm and lights up the child's happy face. The cake has been made and carried to the table by Mother—God—whose beautiful, smiling face radiates unconditional love.

She tells her child that this is a special cake in which all ingredients are not blended together. There are countless pun-

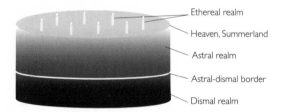

Along the border between the dismal and the astral, we find people like you and me—people who think, speak, and behave like most people on Earth. Forms, structures, and "geography" (forests and mountains and deserts) of that region are reminiscent of our world. As we descend from the border into the darker and denser realms of slower vibration, we begin to see more and more of the ugly, vile, and malevolent side of human nature in the faces and mannerisms of the residents. Moving upward from the border, we find earth-like worlds that become increasingly beautiful and awe-inspiring, eventually manifesting as perfect paradise worlds in which poweful, loving human beings in spirit manifest subtle forms and structures with their minds. This is the region often called Heaven, or the Summerland, a stunning place that's like frosting on the spirit-world cake.

The astral-dismal border is not really a border at all, as the dismal realm blends into astral realm. We call it a border as it is the arbitrary point at which there is a balance between creative and destructive qualities of human nature. I believe it is the point from which most ITC contacts occur, and where our spirit friends establish ITC sending stations.

Above the cake we enter the formless ethereal worlds of light beings and ascended masters, represented here by the candles.

A DEEPER LOOK INTO THE WORLDS OF SPIRITS

gent pockets of diverse flavor. Every bite is unique. For every inhabitable climate on earth there is at least one astral region baked into the body of the cake. There are winterlands and forestlands and tropiclands and mountainlands and prairie-lands and countless other lands baked into the cake. For every traditional culture on earth, characterized by unique clothing, language, art, folk songs, dances, and dialect, there is an astral region somewhere in the cake. For every religion and national-ity there is an astral region.

In the course of creating the cake, things were allowed to settle. The lighter, sweeter, more perfect and appealing ingredi-ents rose toward the top. These are the things that tingle chil-dren's taste buds and make them smile. The heavier, unsavory ingredients—bitter alkaloids[4] and heavy liquors that make chil-dren cringe and send babies into spasms—settled to the bot-tom. The top area of the cake and the frosting are rich with thoughts and attitudes of love, trust, empathy, goodwill, and emotional stability. The bottom layers contain bitter pieces of fear, doubt, domination, animosity, greed, lust, envy, prejudice, and addiction. No one really enjoys the taste of the bottom lay-ers of the cake, but some people like to swallow bites quickly to experience the sensations triggered by the poisons.

We humans live in the illusion that the cake was made just for our pleasure. Someday we'll grow up and see that the cake is our destiny—a timeless world far more wondrous than we can imagine. Someday we'll shed the physical body, and we'll merge with the cake. The personality and attitudes and beliefs that have shaped our lifetime will then carry us to a suitable and compatible region inside the cake. So after we die, life goes on with little change, except that we typically find ourselves liv-ing in a subtler world. If our life resumes in the astral realm, it is a lighter and lovelier existence. If our life resumes in the dis-mal realm, it is a darker and uglier existence.

---

[4] Alkaloids are the notorious "-ines"—caffeine, nicotine, cocaine, morphine, and so on.

Chapter Eight

THE JOURNEY HOME

Now that we've taken a brief look at the classification of realms, let's get an idea of life on the other side by taking a journey through the worlds of spirit.

For this example, imagine you are old and gray, lying in a hospital bed, surrounded by family members. You are ready to leave this world and move to the worlds of spirit. The mind fades out of conscious awareness. The physical body enters a peaceful state of rest as brain activity slows from about twenty to ten vibrations per second. The brain has switched off its input from the five senses, and the spirit body and mind take over.

You're dreaming now. It's something you've been doing all your life, almost every night, but especially in the past few days as you slowly prepare for the transition from earthly life. Lately you've been spending more and more time in paradise—that place where people often go when they dream and awaken after they die—and less time in earthly surroundings. The two worlds begin to overlap, and it's not clear which is the more real.

Across the room you see the wall start to shimmer like heat waves. It captures your attention as a hole the size of a basketball opens up in the wall and quickly grows into a doorway.

(Your family members can't see any of this happening.) Light streams into the room through the doorway, and in steps a small contingent of beaming people. One of them is your favorite grandfather who died many years ago. He's like all the others—young and vital. They surround the bed, assure you that there's no need for alarm, and help you to sit up, then stand up. As you're escorted toward the doorway, you look back and see your lifeless physical body on the bed. You look down, puzzled, and see an exact, living, duplicate body, wearing the same hospital gown. Entering the doorway, you find yourself in a tunnel, amazed by the beautiful rainbow colors pulsing along the walls. The tunnel is like a large, living umbilicus of light. In moments you seem to be moving at tremendous speed, but with no discomfort from friction or wind. Moments later you emerge in a meadow that's so beautiful that it takes your breath away. Distant mountains tower toward the sky, while nearby flowers and trees have a glow about them. The flowers shine from within and seem to be aware of your approach. As they sense your deep appreciation for their beauty, they lean toward you and emit not just heavenly scents, but also celestial music. Butterflies with wings the size of storybooks flutter by and settle on the flowers.

You approach a nearby stream, kneel down, and admire the crystal purity of the water. You scoop up a handful, take a sip, and feel a gentle surge of vitality pass through you. You drop the rest of the water back into the stream and notice that your hand is not wet as it would be on earth. Intrigued, you scoop up a handful of dirt from along the riverbank. It's like a fine and perfect sand as you hold it, but when you let it drift out of your hand, the sand consolidates as part of the soil that provides a firm anchor for the perfect plants that grow in profusion. There are no weeds, only pleasing, compatible flowers, shrubs, and trees.

Overwhelmed by the beauty of this place, you begin to run through the meadow, arms outstretched. The hospital gown has magically disappeared, and you're now wearing attractive and comfortable clothing well suited to paradise and reminiscent of popular clothes during your recent lifetime. Your body is still old, but it feels strong and free of pain.

You're accompanied toward a house that looks just like the home you grew up in—a place of love and happy memories.[5] The white picket fence is lined with friends, relatives, and shopkeepers you knew on earth. All of these people preceded you in death. They're all cheering you on in a fine homecoming celebration. Mom and Dad are on the porch, smiling warmly. It's obvious that any issues and troubled memories between you are long forgotten. There is only a welcoming love. After a happy reunion, they invite you to lie down on a sofa. Suddenly you feel weary, and you fall into a deep, rejuvenating sleep that lasts about six weeks of earth time.

You awaken refreshed and more vital than you can remember. You get up, look in a mirror, and see a young face smiling back; you have a full head of rich hair, but not a trace of blemishes. It's the way you looked at the prime of life. You notice a closet and look in. It's full of clothes—some familiar and earthlike, and some better suited to this paradise world. You think of a nice blue outfit that you had especially liked on earth, but it's not there in the closet. You close the door and reopen it—and *voila!* There it is.

After a few days you begin to feel a pressure in your mouth, and a full set of strong teeth grow in. After a few weeks you're in a perfect body at the prime of life. Injuries will heal quickly, and you will never get sick.

---

[5] Awakening in a spirit-world copy of your childhood home in the presence of your loving parents is a common afterlife scenario, but by no means the only possibility. As long as we lead a decent life with a caring attitude toward others, we'll awaken in a pleasant place surrounded by loving people.

CHAPTER NINE

A TOUR OF PARADISE

You quickly become acclimated to this wonderful world, and you're introduced to a spirit guide who is knowledgeable, wise, and patient. He almost seems superhuman, but he assures you that he once lived on earth just as you did. Since his death he has worked with enlightened beings to learn how to elevate his spiritual vibration. He tells you that spirit guides can be male or female, people who after their lives on earth worked with spiritual masters to learn how to ascend to finer astral realms. There are also ethereal guides who have no gender.

The moment you meet him, you know you can trust him with your innermost thoughts—you can trust him with your life. You sit with your guide and someone else—an even wiser, more magnificent being. You can't tell if this great being is male or female. Your guide tells you it is an ethereal being. He or she leads you through a brief review of your recent lifetime, projecting the events of your life on a screen in front of you, as your guide waits patiently. It seems to take only a few seconds to relive all the significant events of your life. You see the many good things you did to help people, and you see your mistakes. You watch the movie with interest, feeling a small sense of gratification here, a small twinge of regret there.

When it's over, your guide prepares you for a tour of the spirit worlds. You leave the house, and your guide points to a large building in the distance. He takes your hand, and in the next instant you are standing in front of that building. He says it was created by a team of specialists—men and women who on earth had been architects and who had carried their skill along with them after they died. They were told that this would be a library—a hall of records—so they had created plans for a building that would suit the purpose.

As a crowd gathers, your guide explains that those same architects are now going to build an addition, and these events always attract an interested crowd. You ask how exactly they will build it, as there are no building materials or trucks or bulldozers around. Your guide laughs and says it doesn't work that way here.

"Watch," he says as the architects stand at various spots, looking at the side of the library where the addition is to be created. Suddenly a beam of rainbow light forms, shining down on them from some invisible source. At the same time, smaller beams emanate from the heads and bodies of the architects and come together at the chosen site. The structure begins to materialize, and over a period of minutes it becomes more solid and intricate in design. Your guide tells us that the large beam comes from ethereal beings who inhabit worlds beyond form and structure, and it is transduced and filtered by the individual minds here in front of you. "These are brilliant ethereal beings," our guide says, pointing up to the sky, "who provide virtually unlimited creative potential, which is then put to use by the minds of the architects."

When the building is complete, you encounter a small group of friendly strangers. They are going to a concert at a nearby hall and invite you to join them. Some of them are dressed in robes, which are prevalent here in paradise; each robe has its own subtle hues and designs that seem perfectly suited for its owner.

Since there are many of you, it's easier and more enjoyable to walk to the concert hall than to travel by thought. You pass by magnificent gardens of flowers, some of which resemble earthly flowers and can be picked; others are far more intricate and colorful than anything on earth, and your guide warns you that those flowers must not be picked. They are living residents of paradise. The gardens have been planted and nurtured by spirit-world gardeners, again with the creative support of ethereal beings.

Soon you arrive at the concert hall. One of the most vital and basic human endeavors in paradise is music, your guide tells you, though on earth it is often regarded as merely a nice pastime. In paradise, music entwines with all of the sensual beauties. Flowers, streams, and even the things that on earth are seen as inanimate emit music. Not only are the hills alive with music, but buildings and oceans are as well. People who were musically gifted on earth can learn heavenly techniques and other-worldly instruments that make the finest compositions on earth sound rather crude and simple. Physical ears simply are not equipped to hear the harmonies and subtle tones of celestial music. Gifted musicians new to paradise are sometimes overwhelmed by the tremendous possibilities open to them as they slowly learn the complex techniques employed to compose music.

You move your attention now to the symphony orchestra, which is starting to play a soul-stirring composition. As it performs, the concert hall glows in the softest of colors. This light is produced automatically by the music, and it forms magnificent structures of rainbow color above the hall. The light washes through all the spectators, stirring their souls and nourishing their subtle bodies in ways that people on earth can't even imagine.

Next you accompany your guide to an art gallery, where you are introduced to two attractive European women wearing elegant nineteenth-century dresses. Susannah Lehnhoff and

Honorine Deviane[6] were married to famous men during their lifetime (Edouard Manet and Jules Verne, respectively), and now the two women are talented artists in paradise. They show you great masterpieces that have been created here in paradise. The works of art all capture living beauty in a way that eludes their counterparts on earth. You can feel the spirit of the art pieces and even touch them, as well as view them, as they are impervious to damage and decay. Inspirations of the artists are transferred to the media mainly through thought and intention rather than muscular patterning. As a result, the artist can achieve a level of perfection impossible on earth. Free from ego, free from illusions that distort the self-worth of so many on earth, artists instantly know the genuine quality of their work. So there is no contention or competition to have one's artwork on display in the galleries. The works speak for themselves.

Then you're off to a hall of science, where you meet Albert Einstein, Tom Edison, Marie Curie, Henri Sainte-Claire de Ville, and a host of other scientists. Curie tells you that halls of science contain all of the important inventions and discoveries ever devised on earth, plus futuristic inventions that could quickly transform modern civilization. Many of the latter have never been allowed to manifest on earth because of mankind's track record of destruction. Science and technology have always amplified human nature—the best of man and the worst of man, the creative side and the destructive side. The great inventions are ready and waiting for a corresponding peaceful, loving readiness in the earth world. Then subtle minds in paradise worlds will plant seeds of brilliant innovation into receptive minds on earth. That's how the greatest advances have always come to earth in the field of science, as well as in literature, art, music, and so on.

[6] In 1994 an image of a deceased French girl named Anne de Guigne was received in Luxembourg. She was active on the other side, helping children who were suffering on earth. Her picture was a TIF file planted on a computer while no one was home. An accompanying message explained that it had been created by these two French women in the spirit world by a method similar to oil painting on earth.

You ask your guide about famous leaders on earth. What happens to them when they die? He tells you that leaders of politics, religion, business, and other institutions that affect the well-being and destiny of many people can find tremendous rewards after death, or they might find self-imposed punishment, depending on how they used their power and influence on earth and with what intention. Those with a genuine concern for the less fortunate, those who helped spread truth and love, those who fostered trust and goodwill among people—those leaders are celebrated in paradise and welcomed with open arms. Those who caused pain indiscriminately to achieve gain, those who gave of their wealth only if they received a profit or other benefit, those who sacrificed truth and compassion while adhering to rigid and incorrect dogmas and ideologies, those who lost sight of their soul missions—those leaders awaken after death with a gnawing remorse, a frustrating realization that they made mistakes. After death they are driven to compensate, to try to correct the problems they had caused.

Your guide says it's time to leave your new paradise homeland, to start descending in vibration through the various astral regions toward the dismal worlds of darkness. As you walk, your surroundings begin to change. Flowers become less prevalent, shrubs begin to take on a dry appearance, and the grass beneath your feet loses its softness. It feels as though you're walking from a Tahitian meadow on a sunny morning into semi-arid foothills in late afternoon. You're still in the astral realm, but it's not as much of a paradise as the place you left. The people you meet are content, but they lack the glowing smiles and sparkling eyes of paradise.

Your guide tells you that you have been traveling through various astral regions that all blend together. You have been traveling not through three-dimensional space, as on earth, but through vibrational levels, regions, or dimensions of existence. You have been lowering your vibrations, which causes you to move into regions of lower vibration. There are no sudden, profound changes in the geography; things just become less and less verdant and joyful.

You come across a large farm or ranch with countless animals that were mistreated on earth by the hand of man. Many were raised as livestock in dreary surroundings toward a slaughterhouse destiny. The animals in spirit are now being tended to by caring humans, learning to trust and love humans, and will eventually migrate to paradise worlds where endless green pastures wave in the Summerland breezes. For now they are still weary and healing.

You come to one particular stable where you find a man busy with a shovel. Your guide tells you that Pope Pius IX forbade the establishment of a Society for the Prevention of Cruelty to Animals (SPCA) in Rome. He decreed that people have no duty to animals, thus justifying the torture of animals in medical experiments. Since his death in 1878, he has been cleaning stables.[7] It wasn't a punishment imposed by some higher authority, your guide explains. When Pope Pius crossed over and saw clearly for the first time the agony and terror suffered by the lab animals, he felt he had no choice but to try to compensate in some small way for the misery caused by his decision.

You continue your journey into regions that seem denser and more rugged, and you pass through various cities and countryside communities that you might well find on earth. You stop in one particular community that your guide says is at the fringes of the astral world. There is a great deal of work going on here in a project to rescue people.

"Rescue them from what?" you wonder.

"Well, let's have a look," your guide replies.

You come to a building that looks like an immense earthly hospital, with dozens of wings, each of which treats more than

---

[7] In a long computer letter received from the The Seven ethereal beings in Luxembourg on April 3, 1996, cattle madness was likened to human madness. The Christian and scientific view that animals have no souls and can be tortured unconsionably has brought humanity to a dark period in its evolution, they said, and an "education" similar to that of Pope Pius IX is awaiting many others now alive on earth.

a thousand patients. There are literally millions of people in need of rescue, your guide says, and that's why hospitals like this one were created here. They are like paradise outposts in the wild, low-vibration fringes of the astral world. The grounds around the hospital and other buildings in this community are enhanced with parks, creeks, waterfalls, gardens, and sculpted bushes. It's all reminiscent of the higher paradise, but geared more toward earthlike patterns of behavior. There are places where people can enjoy feasts or sexual encounters, whereas in the higher reaches of paradise, in the finer astral worlds, most such activities no longer play an important role in people's lives.

Also, in the finer astral worlds, it's natural to be of service to others, to be selfless, to share the love of all the people around you, and to carry an air of gratitude and praise for higher spiritual ideals, whereas here in the fringes of lower vibrations it's a concerted effort to keep people enthusiastic about spiritual pursuits, much as it is on earth. In this lower-level community, there are frequent sessions or services in which everyone shows their gratitude to God and to higher spiritual beings who observe, guide, and protect them. There are occasional rebellions in which one or two individuals, or maybe a small group of people, decide that earthly patterns (feasting, sex, and diversions) are actually more important and more fun than spiritual patterns of service and supporting God's plan. So it takes a concerted effort of spiritual hierarchies to maintain order and keep people in harmony with the spiritual purpose of the community. That's the only way that these well-ordered outposts can be sustained—through spiritual practices among the inhabitants.

As you enter the spirit-world hospital, your guide tells you that the main tasks here include finding people who are stuck in the dark spirit worlds close to the earth after they have died, extracting them from their situations, bringing them to the hospital, and nursing them back to health in their spirit bodies. That psychospiritual and emotional healing process can take weeks or months of earth time. The patients are fed luscious fruits and savory soups that are actually packaged energy, highly nourishing and sustaining.

Some of the workers in the hospital stay here to help the patients heal, and others travel deep into the dark worlds to locate, assist, and watch over the people who are stuck. These mission workers are bombarded by negative thought forms constantly during their travels, so when they return to the outpost, they too need to consume lots of rejuvenating fruits and drinks to replenish their spiritual vitality.

You visit a patient in the hospital named Arthur M.[8] He and three other German soldiers died near the end of World War II while hitching a ride in a farmer's carriage near Cologne, Germany, in 1945. Arthur says he arrived here at the paradise outpost only recently, and he says he still wakes up in terror, soaked in sweat, reliving the yellow-red blast that lifted the carriage and hurled it to the war-ravaged earth. Suddenly everything went black and silent, Arthur remembers, and he became lost and alone in the darkness. He assumed he had died, but he was confused and had no idea how many earth years were passing. Before long he heard beautiful music in the distance and saw a glowing violet spiral. He felt himself being pulled slowly toward that light, and as he entered it, suddenly he found himself in a paradise valley, the sheer beauty of which caused him to break down sobbing and pass out. That was some fifty years after his tragic death. When he awakened in the lush grass that was covered by morning dew, a friendly young man said, "Welcome, Arthur, we were expecting you!"

Your guide explains to you that a technical group not far from the hospital has been experimenting with equipment that can locate certain individuals in the darker worlds and raise their vibration in a process called light modulation. That's how Arthur was rescued.

---

[8] A computer letter was received in Luxembourg on July 7, 1997, from this fellow, whose aged wife, Lucy, was still alive. She was upset when she learned about the contact from her long-dead husband. To protect her privacy I decided not to publish his last name.

A DEEPER LOOK INTO THE WORLDS OF SPIRITS

You leave the hospital and, propelled by thought, suddenly find yourself in an isolated campsite in a winter-like environment. There are patches of snow on the ground, and the air, although cool, is not uncomfortable. Two men are sitting on rocks—one dressed in animal skins, the other in a suit and tie. Your guide tells you that these two men meet here occasionally because their paths once crossed at an important time. The man clothed in animal skins introduces himself to us as a Dane named Skjoldung. He had been a Viking poet on earth twelve hundred years ago, he says, and since then has been living happily in a small village in the "snow land" of this astral world, which is within traveling distance of the Summerland. One day in 1986, earth time, Skjoldung says he was surprised to find a strangely dressed man lying on the ground, with two wounds dripping blood into the snow. The wounds quickly healed, the man's agony faded away, and he began to ask where he was, where Stockholm was, and where Lisbeth was. Skjoldung says he knew nothing of Stockholm or Lisbeth and could not answer. After the healed man calmed down, he introduced himself as Olof Palme, the world leader and Swedish prime minister who had been assassinated on February 28, 1986, in Stockholm.[9]

Prime Minister Palme, in his suit and tie, smiles and nods, as though to confirm the story. He says he meets with his friend Skjoldung from time to time to hear the story of his awakening here after his death. He remembers joking with Skjoldung after he had been nurtured back to health in the poet's village.

"I told my friend I was ready to go out and find the Summerland, despite the fact that I'm a politician," Palme tells us, "but I don't think Skjoldung caught the humor."

(You catch the humor as you recall that many people on earth call the Summerland heaven and regard politics as a dirty business, not worthy of such a place.)

[9] A computer letter from the ancient Dane poet Skjoldung, written by the spirit of nineteenth-century English explorer Richard Francis Burton, arrived in a Luxembourg computer on February 28, 1996. It reported Olof Palme's awakening in the snow-land of the spirit worlds.

Skjoldung nods and says, "Everyone in our village respects this man. So we imagine a politician must be some kind of great prince or king in the country where Olof Palme came from."

The next place you visit is a tavern. Your guide tells you that many people who die on earth cross over with addictions to alcohol and drugs. The spirit worlds have no substances that can destabilize the central nervous system of the spirit body with mind-altering effects. But here in this tavern, people can drink large glasses of beer, which might look and taste like pale pilsner, but is actually a form of packaged energy that nourishes and recharges the spirit bodies.

One fellow in the tavern has visible remnants of deep psychological troubles. Under his eyes you can see dark circles, which he tells you have been fading since he was brought here. He also has pale, ulcerated skin that shows signs of slow healing.

He says that just a few weeks ago he was trapped in a dark world where he and his drinking buddies would enter taverns on earth, unbeknownst to the clientele. They'd wait for drunken men and women to pass out, then they'd walk right into their bodies to experience the buzz of alcohol and drugs. These are sensations they could no longer get without a physical body, except by entering the bodies of living addicts as spiritual parasites. It was a desperate experience, an unending search for host addicts on earth, and traveling through dark, depressing spirit worlds between encounters.

Finally, this man had had enough. Drained of all energy, he cried out for help, and three beings were by his side almost immediately to escort him to the hospital. Now he has just been released from the hospital and is enjoying new friendships in the tavern. You're apprehensive as your guide tells you that you are now going to visit those dark worlds, but he assures you that you'll be perfectly safe as long as you stay together.

CHAPTER TEN

✼

JOURNEY TO THE DARK SPIRIT WORLDS

You leave the spirit-world tavern, enter the semi-arid region at the fringes of the astral realm, then continue on to worlds of denser vibration in the dismal realm. You notice that there is no clear boundary between the astral and dismal realms; they simply blend together here in the area of this convalescent community.

All vegetation is soon gone. The world becomes barren, gray, and misty. There's a dismal mood hanging over this realm. People are sitting on rocks and on the bare ground and have no idea you're present. They can't see or hear you because your fine and subtle vibration makes you invisible. They have not yet worked through their patterns of troubled thinking and are not yet ready to be rescued.

The people here sit with heads lowered—some weeping, some shaking their heads slowly back and forth and gnashing their teeth, and some uttering streams of profanity. These people are punishing themselves for all sorts of reasons, your guide says. Many feel guilty for bad spiritual choices—perhaps losing sight of the fact they had chosen a lifetime on earth in order to pursue a particular purpose. Instead they became immersed in material wealth and worldly pleasures. Others had caused pain and suffering in people's lives. Still others believed in false dogmas about eternal damnation, and the fear and guilt they carried to the deathbed pulled them like a homing signal to this world of low vibration. Your guide explains that many people on earth die with strong fears, doubts, resentments, and animosities. If they can't wash away some of those troubled feelings either before or after their transition, their spirit will vibrate slowly, so they become trapped here for awhile.

There is always hope, before and after they die, your guide says. While alive on earth, if they recognize mistakes they've made, animosities they've harbored too long, or fears that have gnawed away at their spirit, they can simply ask for the help of ethereal intercessors. They can pray for help, for guidance, for courage and strength. If they ask in earnest, with new attitudes and a commitment to behavior patterns that reflect those new attitudes, they will very likely be pulled up to a finer spiritual vibration before they die.

If people die with a low spiritual vibration, still there is hope, as everyone eventually moves on from the dark worlds into the light. Everyone eventually returns home to paradise. But first these people have to process their patterns of thought and feeling and to find that spark of love and decency inside them. At that point they can be rescued by one of the many astral-realm teams who tour these dark, dismal regions looking for lost souls who are ready to come home to paradise.

Your guide tells you that you are now going to participate in one of those rescues, and within moments you encounter a pretty girl sitting on a rock. Her beauty seems out of place in this world, and you ask her why she is here. She begs you not to hate her when she tells you, and your guide assures her that you are here only to help.

She said she was a beautiful child with a flare for adventure. She begged her parents to let her attend a faraway college until they finally gave in. She entered college in high hopes of becoming a doctor and having a lot of fun in the process. She found herself hopelessly attracted to a handsome young man who was self-confident and charismatic, but who had left a trail of heart-broken friends and lovers. His only interest was to take from people whatever he could take.

At first he ignored this beautiful young freshman girl, because he knew that would make her even more excited. And it did. Once they became lovers, he made her buy him drugs. Eventually he made her bring girls to him, introducing him as a trusted family friend. He would make love to the girls, take their money, then leave them. This pretty girl was unable to leave this terrible relationship. She quit school after the first year and became a waitress. Her parents were horrified when they visited her, and they implored her to return home. She refused.

She was under the control of the dark-spirited man. He collected proof that she had purchased illegal drugs. When he married a homely heiress a year later, he told his girlfriend to kill his young wife. She was horrified by the thought, but he ignored her pleading and threatened to turn her into the police as a drug dealer if she didn't comply.

She realized at that moment she had ruined her life, and she decided that the next morning she would turn herself and him into the police. He could sense a change in her mood, so that night he killed his wife himself. He framed his girlfriend for the murder, and early the next morning he turned her into the police. At the police station she committed suicide. She awakened moments later in this dark, barren landscape and realized that she was in hell. She quickly began to pray in earnest and to cry for help.

Your guide tells you that the ethereal beings heard her cries, and that's why you and he are here now—to help her if you can.

After she has related her story, she says she can't understand why she gave into that man's diabolic plans and was unwilling or unable to free herself. All she knows is that she was trapped by her feelings, and she gradually felt her spirit grow darker and darker, until it was too late.

Your guide tells her that renouncing the dark and accepting the light can usually be achieved much more quickly on earth than here in the spirit worlds. It often takes much time and committed effort for people trapped in the dark spirit worlds to work their way toward the light, but in her case ethereal beings said there were mitigating circumstances that would allow her to be taken to one of the hospitals. Those circumstances include her basic goodness, from which she had lost her way for a year. Suddenly a rescue team arrives and escorts the girl away. "Her boyfriend will not be so fortunate," your guide says. "He will soon die, and he will remain in the darkest, most grotesque realm for ages."[10] As you continue through this dreadful realm you come across a large metal chamber the size of a house. There are people and animals standing outside, peering distastefully through the small, dirty windows. From inside the chamber you can hear muffled screams and groans.

You peek reluctantly into one of the windows and see an immense crowd of people gasping in sheer misery. One man stands out. He's wearing a World War II military uniform. Your guide tells you about Rudolf Hoess (not to be confused with Adolf Hitler's deputy Rudolf Hess). Hoess joined the Nazi secret service in 1934 and was commandant of Auschwitz, the Nazi death camp, from 1940 to 1943. After his execution in Poland in 1947, he was confronted with the unimaginable pain, terror, and death his decisions inflicted on tens of thousands of Jews. Since then he has been in this dark world, haunted by the incessant screams of mothers and the death rattle of their children. Hoess cries for help, saying, "The air is filled with gas. Please help us by praying. Sixty-five thousand spirits cry and scream. Their bodies are too heavy for us. . . . Please stay away from

---

[10] How do we avoid a fate such as these suffered by people in the dismal realm? Techniques are provided in Chapter 18.

teachings of racial superiority. Many want to help us, but the doors are closed. We are being observed by animals through observation holes. Where is God? Far away there are white roses in bright light. If we could reach those roses we would be free. Please pray for our freedom, for we deeply regret our deeds. This is Rudolf Hoess."[11] You are at the same time moved and repulsed by the sounds of terror, and your guide explains that those suffering are primarily the murderers, stuck in a horrific moment in time with spiritual echoes of the victims of the Nazi gas chambers. After some soul-searching you ask your guide if there is some spiritual significance to the white roses.

"There is political and moral significance," your guide says. "White Rose was a German resistance movement whose right-minded members worked against Hitler and the Nazi atrocities. So using symbology of that era, the White Rose would be akin to paradise, while Nazi crimes represent the dismal side of humanity." The guide doesn't know who created the symbol in this gas-chamber hell, but it was probably formed by the minds and memories of the suffering inhabitants.

You ask if there's anything you can do to help these miserable people. Your guide says that until they have worked through the guilt, torment, and terror from their earth experience, only so much can be done to free them. There is one thing, your guide says, and it involves people on earth.

"These poor wretches here in the dismal realm might not be able to see higher spiritual beings like us, but they are aware of people on earth. When people on earth pray for them, streams of higher vibration wash over them. Love and decency suddenly light up their dark world, and in those moments they can see the spirit-world missionaries who have come to help them.

<hr>

[11] This contact from Rudolf Hoess was received in 1996 by ITC researcher Adolf Homes of Germany. Home's prolific ITC results have been documented by ITC expert Ernst Senkowski, retired physics professor at the University of Mainz and founder of the Institute of Psychobiophysics.

At that point they can be rescued. If people on earth don't help, then these lost souls can remain lost for centuries of earth time."

As you pull yourself away from this scene of misery, your guide says you could go still deeper, into worlds that are dark and ugly almost beyond description, where people with grotesque, misshapen bodies impose unimaginable tortures on each other, especially on those who are consumed by fear. Your guide reiterates that leaving the earth enmeshed in negative attitudes (resentment, bitterness, fear . . .) can trap spirits in low vibration and pull them deep into the dismal realm. You're relieved that you won't go there. "You get the picture," your guide says with a wistful look. "It's time to return home."

As you begin the trip back to paradise, your guide informs you that rescue work, especially in the darkest of worlds, is among the most dangerous of jobs in paradise. Rescuers have to remain objective in their thoughts. Empathetic and sympathetic feelings can drag down the rescuers' vibrations. If they begin to share the sadness, guilt, or fear of those who are stuck in darkness, then they themselves can get stuck too. So rescuers are taught to remain even tempered and on task.

As you return to the hospital at the fringes of the astral realm, your guide tells you that the rehabilitation of lost souls means changing their thoughts and attitudes from dismal (looking away from God) to astral (looking toward God). It suddenly occurs to you that life on earth is unique. People are jumbled together in the same place—within families, within communities, and within one world—but they do not remain distinct by their frequency or vibration. Almost every day on earth you encounter some people who are loving and trusting and others with dark motives that might or might not be apparent.

Your guide smiles broadly. "That's right," he says. "That's the amazing aspect of life on earth. You have the opportunity to move very quickly toward God, because there are many people of fine spiritual vibration to help you and provide good examples."

More somberly he continues, "By the same token, you can move very quickly away from God by making bad choices on earth—choices that hurt the people around you and take you away from your life purpose. In any case, at the end of your earthly life you have developed a certain spiritual vibration by the choices you've made during your lifetime. Your spiritual vibration can carry you into the astral realm for a paradise existence or into the dismal realm for a wretched existence. And once you're in the spirit worlds, you find yourself surrounded by people who think and behave much the way you do. As a result, there are few opportunities to adjust your spiritual vibration after you die."

"So accepting a life on earth is a gamble."

"Yes, it is," your guide replies. "Souls can come to earth with the best of intentions, to raise their vibration, to use that lifetime to move themselves to finer astral worlds by leading a loving life of service and compassion. But if they get sidetracked by the many earthly temptations—getting rich at other people's expense, getting lost in drugs, alcohol, sexual promiscuity, and so on—then they can actually lower their vibrations and wind up in a more dismal world after they die. And then they're stuck there. Spiritual progress is very slow once you're in the spirit worlds, especially in the darker, dismal levels where no one is thinking about spiritual advancement, where everyone's lost in their troubled thinking. And that's why this rescue project is so important. It provides a rare chance for many lost souls, who have made bad choices on earth, to find redemption."

After a pause, your guide says that a new form of community is needed today: a community both on earth and in the astral realm, focused on the well-being of the earth and humanity at large—a sort of spiritual United Nations made up of men and women of goodwill.[12] This community on both sides of the veil would work in conjunction with the various religious, national, and tribal communities that flourish in the astral worlds and on earth. The larger, all-encompassing community—the alliance between heaven and earth—will support them.

"That's God's plan for this world—the reclamation of humanity by the forces of light—and ITC is a part of that plan," your guide says.

---

12 Such an interfaith, interworld community was established a half-century ago by my friend Juliet Hollister with the help of former First Lady Eleanor Roosevelt and with ethereal help. Since Juliet's death, the earthly side of her Temple of Understanding has continued in the capable hands of Alison van Dyk.

CHAPTER ELEVEN

TO THE EDGE OF THE ETHEREAL REALM

Your guide says it's time to return to the higher paradise, from where you'll embark on your final journey. You find yourself suddenly back at your home. You're once again overwhelmed by the sheer beauty of this place, and you're still amazed by this ability to travel by thought. Your guide explains that people here in paradise can learn thought-traveling without too much trouble, since it is a natural process at the finer levels of existence, as is creating forms by thought. Newcomers feel a sense of power and freedom as they develop these skills.

With practice, your guide says, individuals can use their focused thoughts to control the speed and direction of large spirit-world vehicles—ships, airplanes, buses, and so on, which might carry many passengers. The pilots often feel a tremendous sense of power and gratification while controlling those vehicles.

Now you are going to travel into finer vibrations where mental creativity grows increasingly powerful. To your delight, you are joined by three magnificent beings who glow in rainbow colors. Your guide tells you that when ethereal beings visit the astral realm, their powerful energies are transduced down so as not to blind or bother the paradise people. These beings emit purity, knowledge, and wisdom. They're like a bank of living supercomputers that exchange oceans of information instantly. Normally they exist as pure consciousness without form, and it is only when they descend in vibration to enter the astral realm that they take on these bodies you see.

In their presence you feel like a child sitting on its mother's lap. You begin to move at a fast but comfortable pace into regions that become increasingly light, colorful, and mystical. You are passing through the highest reaches of the astral realm. There are crystal palaces tucked away in pristine forests alive with the colors of the rainbow, plus hundreds of brilliant hues that are beyond the range of human eyes. As forms become lighter and more elegant, you suddenly come to an invisible barrier. The ethereal guides explain that this is the boundary between form and formlessness. Beyond it is the ethereal realm, their home.

They ask you to close your eyes and relax, and within moments you feel yourself leave your astral body and enter a state of pure bliss. Suddenly you seem to have a more complete knowledge and understanding than you ever would have thought possible. All of creation now seems to make sense as you melt with the elements and lose all track of time and space and form. It seems like no time at all before you are gently pulled out of your bliss and back into your astral body. It feels like you have just come out of a dream, and your astral body seems rather heavy. You can only imagine how dense, thick, and heavy a physical body would feel right now.

Your guide tells you that in the ethereal realm, thousands of years on earth can pass by in a heartbeat, so whenever astral residents visit the ethereal realm, it always feels as though they are shaken gently out of their reverie far too soon.

After the journey you wonder why humans don't avoid all that drama of the dismal and astral worlds. Why don't we move straight to the ethereal realm after we die? You suggest to your guide that if people moved back close to the Source, where everything is blissful and perfect, wouldn't that be nicer and easier?

Your guide says that's impossible. The patterns of time, space, gravity, and structure and other illusions become so deeply etched in the mind during a lifetime on earth that you can't simply release them and move on to a more ethereal existence. Rather, you have to process those patterns gradually in the astral realm after a life on earth—or actually, after many lifetimes on earth. As you release those patterns, you move into subtler, finer astral worlds. Once those patterns are gone, you can finally move beyond the realms of form and structure into the ethereal realm.

CHAPTER TWELVE

SPIRITUAL INSIGHTS OFFER
"REAL WORLD" PERSPECTIVE

We often think of our familiar surroundings here on earth as the real world and of spiritual existence as something abstract and unreal. My research indicates the opposite is true; the closer we move toward the Source, the more purity we encounter in knowledge and understanding. It is the densest vibrations here in the physical realm that make up the most *unreal* and illusory world.

In the course of a lifetime we develop patterns of physical-world living in our minds. How smoothly we can move on to paradise depends largely on how quickly we can trade those familiar patterns for patterns of spiritual reality.

Knowledge of the following spiritual concepts can help our minds begin to develop those spiritual patterns now, while we are alive on earth, so that when we die, we will not awaken in a world that seems strange or struggle and panic while we try to figure out where we are. Instead, we will know that we've come home to paradise.

Contact field. Our spirit friends have told us that ITC depends on what they call a *contact field,* a pool of life energy composed of the thoughts and attitudes of all the researchers involved in an ITC project, and also the thoughts and attitudes of their spirit group. That field of consciousness spans many dimensions. Although the contact field remains invisible and undetectable to us on earth, our spirit friends can see it the way we might see a mist on a cool, damp morning. When everyone's thoughts are in harmony, the contact field is clear. They can see into our world and work with our equipment. But if there is dissonance in the form of fears, doubts, and animosities, the contact field becomes cloudy, and it is impossible for them to see into our world and work with us. That's when negative spirit groups close to the earth in vibration can break into existing bridges, with troubling results. Troubled feelings seem to open the field to troubled spirit worlds as they close down the field to the finer worlds.

The celestial plan for the earth seems to be to bring together all the dark and light qualities of humanity for a complete healing and thus restore paradise to the physical realm. We are told there was a paradise in our distant past; it served as inspiration for the biblical Eden but was not quite as depicted in ancient religious texts. (The fascinating story of our ancient heritage is a subject of Chapter 16.)

Resonance. As spirit friend Konstantin Raudive told us through a radio set in 1994, "It can only work when the vibrations of those present are in complete harmony, and when their aims and intentions are pure." Collaboration among realms or dimensions requires harmony among all those on both sides of the veil.

Resonance or harmony is a natural way of life for our friends in the worlds of spirit. In the spirit world, things and people come together when they're in harmony. Spirits of like mind simply find themselves in each other's company.

But it's not easy to achieve and sustain harmony among a group of people here on earth. In the coming decades ITC researchers will work on techniques to sustain a degree of harmony among a group of people over a period of time. It involves overcoming our fears, doubts, envy, and animosities, and learning to work selflessly with others in trust and friendship.

Resonance is a state of going with the flow. When vibration is synchronized, less and less energy is required to excite the system. Pure resonance allows a system, once vibrating, to keep vibrating indefinitely. Theoretically, resonance among a group of humans on earth could be a self-sustaining force, once the techniques to achieving genuine harmony are mastered. That is rarely achieved outside of monasteries and cloisters.

Decency. Our spirit friends from the finer levels of spirit—the ethereal beings—tell us that decency plays an important role in establishing a good contact field. Here are messages delivered by our ethereal friends to our INIT research group. (The messages have been translated into English and condensed, but care has been taken to preserve the original meaning.)

God is everything, so it doesn't matter which religion you accept. Universal truth is found along the path of decency, which is found through honesty. Committing to eternal principles opens the doors to freedom.

Many of you want to prove ITC's legitimacy, but most of the tests available in your present world are inadequate. The phone taps you arrange with the telecommunications companies provide only a partial picture of what is really happening during phone contacts from us.[13] The bottom line is honesty and

---

[13] Adolf Homes of Germany and other European researchers have instructed the phone companies (for example, Deutsche Telekom) to install and monitor dedicated phone lines with unpublished phone numbers for specific periods of time. In all cases, the only phone calls received on those lines were from the spirit team, and the phone company reported that no calls were made on those lines. The only logical conclusion: The calls did not come through the public networks. Instead, our spirit friends set up their equipment in invisible realms, directly next to or supermposed over our equipment. That confirms our premise that the spirit worlds are right here, all around us.

sincerity on the part of ITC researchers. Without honesty, there can be no legitimate ITC.

A true ITC researcher tries to get contacts through various apparatuses, but successful results are no more important to us than the spiritual growth you experience along the way. We view your world and your efforts through spiritual eyes.

Some of you believe an eternal spark—a piece of God—resides within everyone, and through this flame all people on earth could achieve oneness in their relationships and rapports. This is not entirely true. Being in a physical body in a physical world, you are subject to the shortcomings and daily struggles that your rugged life entails (created in human lives by such things as hormones, egos, and limited perception through the physical brain). As you know, when you pick up a rock you can sometimes find worms, bugs, and other things that are repulsive to you. Likewise, when you find yourself under the weight of negative feelings such as fear, insecurity, doubt, and envy, repulsive things emerge in the form of hatred and compulsions towards vengeance and destruction. Such negative forces in your world cannot easily be swept aside. You can't make those around you see the "light" simply by trying to appeal to that divine inner core. What you call spiritual growth involves personal commitment to overcome these physical forces.[14]

Dispassier point. Imagine handing out paper and boxes of crayons to a class of kindergartners and asking each child to draw the nicest picture they can draw. When they're done, you

---

[14] Excerpts from a series of contacts from The Seven received between January and June, 1996, through the computer of Maggy Harsch-Fishbach of Luxembourg. Translated with permission of the Harsch Fishbachs by Hans Heckmann. First published in its entirety in *Contact!* (1996, issue 3).

gather all the pictures into a stack, then study each picture for, say, the very reddest shade of red. Then you line up all of the pictures so that all of these red areas on all of the pictures are lined up with each other, one on top of another, so that if you pushed a pin through the stack of papers you could pierce the reddest items on all the papers.

That would be like a *dispassing point* or *dispassier point*, a point at which various spirit worlds or dimensions intersect. If you were to take many dimensions of existence, all flourishing with intelligent life and superimposed over each other, and realign them so that only certain types of people or small groups within each dimension come together in a sort of multidimensional line, then you could establish an ITC bridge upon that point where dimensions cross—at that dispassing point.

Over the years I've tried to trace the words *dispassier* and *dispassing* to some original meaning, possibly in French or Italian, but to no avail. It was simply a term delivered to us by our spirit friends on several occasions, mostly through computers in Europe. Text messages from the other side referred to "dispassier points" or "dispassing points" with little explanation.

Then, in the fall of 2005, as I was writing the final chapters of this book, it struck me. *Dispassion, dispassionate*—removing all fear, anxiety, and animosity; removing all passion, and holding onto a calm, stable resolve. It occurred to me that a dispassionate attitude provides the basis for a stable ITC bridge. If groups and individuals on earth and in the various realms of spirit can come together on an ITC project and collaborate on a basis of calm, loving trust, then the contact field can remain strong and clear, allowing competent spirit teams to move into our homes and labs and to work with our equipment. A calm, detached attitude—what Hindus call *sattwa guna*—is one key to establishing a dispassier point for ITC research.

Light and down modulation. Our ITC friends in paradise tell us they can move among the dimensions—up and down the dispassing point—through processes they call *light modulation* and *down modulation*. To travel to the darker worlds on rescue missions, or to travel to earth to work with our equipment, teams of spirit-world scientists and technicians undergo down modulation, which slows the vibration of their spirit bodies so that they move into denser and denser levels. To return to paradise, they undergo light modulation in order to raise the vibration of their bodies.

They have equipment in their spirit world labs that facilitates this modulation. While the team members travel, technicians back at the lab can monitor their journey and regulate their vibrations so that the team can move to certain locations along the dispassing point. This technical modulation of spirit bodies seems to be a process being developed on the other side with which to interact with technologies in our modern world—especially our communication technologies.

Psycho-spiritual aptitude. Successful ITC researchers—those who get the best results—have a focused will that penetrates the veil. Some people have this psycho-spiritual aptitude, which makes them good candidates for ITC research. A spirit colleague of ours named Yang Fudse says he was a physician in ancient China. Among the things he told us over the years, he said: "In specially suited experimenters (to whom you wrongly refer as successful), there develops a sort of emotional lance in the center of their emotional consciousness, which materializes inaudible and invisible tones, signs, and pictures in your realm. People are usually born with this particular polarization of consciousness. Others may try as hard as they can, [but] they will not get these results."[15]

Evil. After observing many realms of spirit in the course of my research, I'm convinced that evil is like cold and dark. It

---

[15] Excerpt of an extensive contact by Yang Fudse, received in the spring of 1997 through the computer of Maggy Harsch-Fishbach. Translated with permission by Hans Heckmann. Published in *Contact!* (1997, issue 3).

does not really exist except as a human concept. Cold is the absence of heat, dark is the absence of light, and evil seems to be the absence of source light, what is sometimes called holy spirit. Here in the physical realm, our conscious minds are far removed from the source of divine light. We're far removed from the source in vibration, not in time or space. In time and space, light from the source is right here with us, and also inside us. But because we are vibrationally removed, the light becomes dim here, and so pockets of chaos develop in our lives and in our world, a condition that some cultures have labeled "evil."

When we're stuck outside in a blizzard, or groping our way through a room during a power outage at night, it's hard to believe that cold and dark are just illusions or concepts, not real. And when we see the ways in which people sometimes mistreat animals and other people, it's hard to believe that there's no such thing as evil. Be that as it may, source light or holy spirit is a nonvibrating energy, a subtle energy that exists beyond the electromagnetic spectrum. When that energy is ignored or shunned, the result is a condition that we label "evil."

So the traditional dichotomy of good and evil as two opposing forces is incorrect. Simply stated, there is only light from the source (which is good) and an absence of that light (which is not good). This may seem like a small matter of semantics, but its future implications in the evolution of society will be profound, I'm sure.

PART THREE

PUTTING THE KNOWLEDGE TO USE

Most of us alive on earth, in our day-to-day waking lives, are closed down to the many spiritual worlds flourishing with life around us. We are completely immersed in our physical world. As a result, when loved ones die, we are unaware of their continued existence and only vaguely aware of their loving heart connection with us, and so we feel a tremendous sense of loss and separation. In human terms, that translates to grief, which weighs down heavily on our heart. The luminator and other ITC technologies have provided comfort to those suffering a loss. Alleviating grief is just one of many applications for ITC techniques.

CHAPTER THIRTEEN

TIANNA AND WILLIAM

If there were some sort of cosmic library containing a record of human relationships, I believe you could find a picture of Tianna Conte and William Dubs under the terms *unbridled passion* and *twin souls*.

Tianna met William in the late 1980s, when they were both in their thirties, and she describes him as the sexiest and best-looking guy she'd ever met. Thick, black beard and mustache, head full of hair, sparkling eyes complementing a contagious laugh, and a body dripping with charisma and animal magnetism. Tianna bore some deep emotional wounds from age thirteen when, during the funeral of her beloved father, a young man close to the family began to comfort Tianna and ended up raping her. As a result, Tianna was in shock that day and for many months to come, so that she was never able to shed a tear for her father. The incident made relationships difficult for her.

William and Tianna developed a close friendship and working partnership based on trust, respect, and an agreement that it would be a platonic relationship. Besides Tianna's emotional wounds, there were other factors keeping them romantically apart. (You can read all about these in the first book of Tianna's trilogy, *Love's Fire*.) A warm and caring rapport developed between William and Tianna over three years, and they resisted getting physically involved until the temptation became overwhelming. Various forces came into alignment, and they finally became lovers. But they didn't just hop into bed; they spent the day on a beach, listening to the ocean surf and discussing their innermost needs and desires.

Shortly after consummating their love affair, they sat down together and wrote their three golden rules for a loving friendship: (1) their individual needs would not be kept secret, but heard and honored; (2) they would be honest and truthful in all their interactions; (3) the sacred union would last only as long as they were each growing spiritually and becoming more loving and more united, and as long as William's eight-year-old son was benefiting from the relationship. If any of those conditions were broken, they would reevaluate.

The love affair grew stronger and more passionate for the next ten years as their physical and emotional needs were satisfied more fully than either of them could have dreamed possible. They maintained separate homes but lived together about half the time.

Tianna and William enjoyed the most sexually and spiritually gratifying times of their lives. They learned from psychics that they were twin souls. They took vacations together, including a month-long trip to Egypt, during which time they had an overwhelming mystical experience suggesting they both had spiritual roots in the early Egyptian mystery schools.

As they began to talk about marriage, they received the shock of their lives. William was diagnosed with an aggressive form of testicular cancer. His main chance of survival, according to both medical and alternative practitioners, was chemotherapy. But chemotherapy had killed William's father, so he absolutely refused that intrusive treatment. They tried a series of non-traditional therapies, and nothing worked.

By October 1997, things looked bleak. William seemed to be on his death bed, contemplating assisted suicide, but Tianna refused to let William go. They decided to get married that month—probably the last thing William would be able to offer his soul mate. So they were married in a small ceremony— William in his hospital bed, Tianna by his side, and a circle of close friends and family gathered around.

A month later the doctors were stunned when tests indicated that William's organs were functioning again, and the cancer marker had dropped miraculously. It appeared that William was in spontaneous remission. Tianna was once again ecstatic, but William was not, for reasons she could not understand. Despite the medical reports, he felt the life energies were nearly depleted from his body.

By December, William had relapsed. On Pearl Harbor Day he called Tianna to his side and puckered his lips for a kiss. As their lips touched, Tianna's body filled with spiritual light, and she seemed to be pulled out of her body. She and William were traveling through a tunnel and into a brilliant white light. As soon as they reached it, William kept moving, but Tianna returned to her body.

The day after William's death, a psychic told Tianna that William was planning a surprise at his memorial ceremony. A few days later, a large gathering of friends and family converged on the Wainwright House in Rye, New York, to attend William's service and party. During a candle-lighting ceremony, Tianna's hair burst into flames, which were quickly extinguished by her fireman brother-in-law. The following day, Tianna and her sister prepared for the worst as they examined Tianna's hair. Both were shocked to find no damage whatsoever—not a trace of singed or shortened hair. Apparently it had been a blue-orange spirit fire created by William.

A few months later, while Tianna was still devastated by her loss, she attended a Raymond Moody workshop, where one of the participants discussed my work. She was intrigued but a little intimidated by the technology aspect of ITC. William had frequently called her a techno-peasant. He, on the other hand, had been fully immersed in technology and communication; unbeknownst to Tianna, he was already active with an ITC spirit group on the other side and was familiar with my work.

Three years after the Moody workshop, I gave a workshop at the Wainwright House. As Tianna made a mental note of the workshop date, she heard William laugh quietly in her head and say, "Be there." She remained leery but ran the idea by her friend Joyce during a phone call. She told Joyce that she didn't know why William was compelling her to attend.

Joyce replied, "It sounds right to me."

Tianna said, half-jokingly, that if William really wanted her to go, he'd have to give her a sign along with some assurance that he'd provide some kind of other-worldly tech support. The two women laughed, and then the phone suddenly went dead. Tianna tried to call Joyce back several times that evening, but couldn't get through. Eventually Joyce called back, and they both had another good laugh. Tianna conceded. She would attend my workshop.

Hearing of that incident recently, I suspect my spirit group was working with William; they were trying to break into the phone conversation to let William speak. I've learned that our spirit friends make many such efforts, but it is difficult at this time to make such contacts, especially to people who are not directly involved in the ITC research and are not therefore part of the contact field. So there are frequent cases of malfunctioning equipment, as our invisible friends try to break through with ITC contacts. On the evening of my workshop, a blizzard passed over the area and blanketed New York. As snow fell, Tianna became reluctant to leave home, but William insisted. She heard his voice in her mind saying, "Get going!" She asked for a sign, and he replied, "Bring Macy's book." Tianna had no idea where the book was, but William guided her to a particular box. As she opened it, there was the book, right on top.

As she held the book, the phone rang. A friend who was going to the seminar asked Tianna if she wanted a ride. Dazed a bit by the synchronicities, she said yes.

At the workshop, I spent an hour sharing the results of ITC research, then we took a break to take pictures. Tianna told William mentally, "This is your chance. If it's what you've been waiting for, show up. You got me here. Please show up." She heard William's familiar laughter in her head, so she knew he would try.

I took Polaroid pictures one by one and laid them on a nearby table to develop. After Tianna's was taken, she walked to the table and watched with hope. She didn't know what to expect, but she certainly felt William's presence.

As the Polaroid became clearer, I heard a gasp from the table. Tianna was feeling chills running through her body. The photo was beyond anything she could have expected. There was her beloved William, reflected clearly through her own face. William's face was superimposed over Tianna's face, so it appeared that Tianna had a little beard and mustache. The shape of the skull was masculine, and the eye and eyebrow on one side were William's (photo 47 and 48, Tianna).

Tianna turned excitedly to her friend and showed him the picture. He laughed and said, "Leave it to William to be in your face."

Everyone in the group was amazed by several of the excellent pictures we received that night, especially Tianna's picture of William. I asked if anyone wanted a second picture taken, and just about everyone did. This time Tianna's picture came out clear, providing a good comparison (photo 47, Tianna). Today they are treasures in Tianna's growing library of memories of a love that burns even today between heaven and earth.

CHAPTER FOURTEEN

DEBBIE AND JOHN

Debbie Alberti sent me an e-mail in the spring of 2004. Her husband, John, had died three weeks earlier, and she was devastated. Here is what she said:

Dear Mark,

My name is Debbie Alberti. I'm 46 years old and have just recently (March 4, 2004) tragically and suddenly lost my husband, John Alberti who was 50 years old, to what we believe was a massive heart attack. He was taking a tennis lesson, practicing serves, when he fell into the instructor, unconscious, hit the floor, still unconscious and not breathing and never knew what hit him. The police and paramedics could not get a regular heart rhythm back, even after 6 shock treatments. They had a defibrillator on him within 60 to 90 seconds, as the tennis club has trained personnel for these crisis situations.

John and I are both musicians—I'm a singer/songwriter; John is a drummer/songwriter. We were together for 8 years and were married on July 11, 1999.

John was not only my husband, but was also my best friend, favorite companion and soul mate. Our marriage was a second one for both. It was not "love at first sight," but as we got to know each other as friends, we came to "see" and feel our deeper connection and the spiritual purpose of our finding each other.

Our marriage was not perfect, but we lived a conscious relationship, always talking things through and always questioning, reflecting, analyzing in a self-introspective way what our part in a disagreement, conflict, discomfort, dissention was so as to better understand our "issues" and "baggage" so that we could evolve to a different place as individuals, as well as a couple. I feel that John's death was too soon and too sudden—that we were both, as individuals, on the brink of getting to that next level—but that is only my small, human, earth-plane perspective.

We shared the same interests and beliefs of Jungian psychology, metaphysical sciences, paranormal psychology, life after "death," synchronicity, thoughts creating our reality, etc.—just to name a few.

So, it was of no surprise that your name and your work came to me through a mutual friend (of my husband's and mine)—Dr. Steve Martin—who is a Jungian analyst and also a believer of all of the above. Steve has been aware of your work for years and directed me to your website and also suggested your book "Conversations Beyond the Light." I loved your description on your website of the "boggle point." It was described so well.

As open as I believe myself to be, I'm afraid that I may have reached my "boggle point," but am still aware that I don't want to "throw the baby out with the bathwater." So, that's why I'm writing you today—to stretch my "model" a bit farther to accept all the information I've been reading in "Conversations Beyond the Light." An aside, I've been reading afterlife material before I even met John.

Let me get to my point—it's only been three weeks since John's death and I desperately, desperately need to hear from John from the afterlife to know in my heart what my head believes—that John's essence and energy, soul, personality and consciousness is still in existence and that he's happy and at peace. I am questioning the whole purpose of my existence here on earth. To know, truly know, in every cell of my body that John is still alive, will be key to my moving forward with my life.

To communicate with John in some way would not only bring me comfort to this walking, waking nightmare I'm in, but would open my mind and life to a whole new world.

Do you have any suggestions on how I can extend myself here on this plane to help John reach me (as I know he will try to do—does he know about Timestream?). If I have an ideal wish, it would be to meet and work with you (or Maggy and Jules) personally to make this communication. Could that be a possibility?

Mark, I know you must receive thousands of these requests, and I know that grief is a universal experience, but right now my grief is soooo alone and personal. Can you help me? (In helping me, I can help others).

Respectfully,
Debbie Alberti

Meanwhile, Debbie's sister-in-law, Tracie (the wife of John's younger brother, Gregory), had had a remarkable lucid dream, in which John came to her. In her dream, Tracie promised John to convey the message to Debbie and other family members, but when she awakened she had second thoughts. She didn't want to intrude on her grieving sister-in-law's life, and she didn't want Debbie (and the rest of the family) to think she was crazy. It wasn't until nine days later (two days after Debbie's e-mail to me) that Tracie told Debbie of the dream. I requested that Tracie dictate the dream into a recorder, and this is the result:

> I wrote down the experience shortly after the dream so that I could do this for you, Debbie. Even today I can still feel the enthusiasm that John had. It was incredible. It was amazing. Couldn't believe my ears. Couldn't believe my eyes. I don't generally dream, that I know of, and certainly if I do I never remember it. So this was quite unusual for me to remember any of it, and I remember it as if it were just so real.

I remember it happened on the seventeenth of March. I remember waking up at five o'clock in the morning thinking, what the heck just happened, and feeling real weird. I couldn't believe what just happened and how real it felt.

As the dream started, I was talking with my sister, and I'd recently been to the doctor for what they thought was a heart murmur, and I was just discussing with her if she thought I should have it further checked out. I guess I was a little extra concerned because of what had just happened to John. And then things kind of, like, darkened, and all of a sudden, there was John. He had this big grin on his face—I mean this big smile. I can see it as I'm talking to him. I can see that big smile.

He chuckled and he said to me, "What're you worried about? You are so gonna live the best of both worlds." Like he knew something.

And I thought to myself, "This is crazy. My brother-in-law just passed away, and I was just in the midst of talking to my sister. What the heck is going on?" I thought maybe I was crazy, and I think I said it aloud. "Am I crazy?"

Because John replied, "No, you're not crazy. It's really me. But listen to me. I don't have a lot of time. I need you to do something for me."

I'm still looking at him, like, "Yeah, right, okay." John looked at me and said, "Tracie, listen to me, I need your attention. I don't have a lot of time, and I need to tell you a couple of things. I need you to do something for me."

I remember replying, "Okay, what is it you need me to do?"

He said, "Tracie, I need you to be my go-between. I need you to relay a couple of messages."

PUTTING THE KNOWLEDGE TO USE

I thought, "Okay-y-y-y." I remember asking him, "Where are we?"

He didn't really explain to me, but he started to ramble on, and you have to picture him enthusiastic, outgoing, energetic—like, chin in the air, glowing grin on his face. When I look at him, I'm seeing John. He's got his glasses on; he's got the black short-sleeved tee-shirt that I always remember him wearing. It's like probably one of his favorite things, and he just started to go on about this place. "Tracie, in your wildest dreams you can't imagine. You can't imagine this place! Tracie, I have studied all sorts of western and eastern religion, and I've read tons of books. You know I've always been in touch with this kind of stuff, and . . . I can't give you too much information. I'm limited in what I can say to you, but you can't fathom this place. It's just so amazing.

"At first when I got here I was pissed. I couldn't figure out where I was, and then I realized I was lying in bed. In bed, and it was dark, and I was in this room. All I could see was a man sitting next to my bed, and I started to freak out. I started to go crazy. The man told me he was my guide and to not worry, and we had this long discussion. The result is, I had to make a decision to go with what this man told me and walk through this door, or to choose not to. I chose to go through the door. Tracie, I walked through this door, and it was just amazing. I opened the door, and standing at the door was my grandfather—my mother's father. He was standing there with this big grin on his face, like 'John!' And behind him stood my grandmother, and she had tears and a smile on her face. I couldn't believe my eyes. I mean, what the heck was I seeing? I couldn't believe my eyes. I'm looking around and I can't believe what I'm seeing. You know, I've been here for a little while now, and it's like I'm catching up with all these people. My cousin Tony is here, and some friends I've had. All these people! It's amazing. I'm okay."

And his hands are going a mile a minute as he's telling me this story. And he's going on and on about how he was okay, and how amazing it was. He said, "It's beyond what is ever imagined. It's beyond what is ever read. It's amazing. I'm okay, I'm fine."

And all I figured out was, "Hey, are you in heaven? Is it heaven? Does it really exist?" I've always had a question of whether heaven existed, but the way John was going on and on about wherever he was, it was like all of a sudden I didn't fear death anymore. I wasn't afraid of it. It was like *I* wanted to go to wherever *he* was.

And all he could say to me is, "Tracie, listen to me. I can't get into a lot of detail. I'm limited to my information. I can't elaborate. Just trust me, it's absolutely beyond your wildest dreams. Trust me. But what I need for you to do for me, Tracie—and it's important—I need you to be my go-between. I need you to relay a couple of messages."

I was wondering, "John, why me? Why wouldn't you go to your wife? To Debbie? Or your family, or one of your friends? You've got all these friends? Why not go to one of them?"

"Tracie, I picked you. I need you to do it. You're family, but you're removed just enough—you're just enough on the outside so you can handle it. And I know you can handle it. I know you're hearing me. I know you know you're talking to me, and I know that you can do this for me. I need you to do this. It's really important. Promise me that you're gonna do this."

"John, whatever you need me to do, I'll do it." I was kind of like amazed at what I was seeing and hearing and how energetic and enthusiastic he was. I just could not believe my eyes, but, "Whatever you need me to do, I'll do, John, but are you sure you want me to do this?"

"Yes, I trust you. I know you can do it. Just promise me you'll do it. I'm running out of time. Just promise me. Hurry up and promise me."

"Okay, tell me what I'm supposed to do."

Then all of a sudden the enthusiasm left. He gave a little sob and got kind of quiet and mellowed out a little bit. He looked at me and he said, "Tracie, you need to tell my family I'm okay. I mean this. You need to tell them I'm okay. I'm fine. I'm okay, I'm okay, I'm o-kay. I need you to tell them that I love them very much and that I'm okay. Make them believe you, Tracie, make them understand. I can see them, I can hear them. I know everything that you're doing. I'm watching you. I can see it. You just can't imagine this place. I need to hurry up. I'm running out of time. I need you to promise me you're going to tell them that. That I'm okay. I'm o-kay."

I said back to him, "Okay."

He said, "Tracie, the next thing I need you to do …," and he put his hand over his heart, and he held it there. He just rubbed his chest and he held it there, and he said, "You have to tell Debbie. Please tell Debbie I love her with all my heart. With all my heart, and it's not over. She'll understand. Just tell her that. Promise me, Tracie, you'll do this for me. You'll tell my family. Promise me you'll tell Debbie. It's SO important, Tracie, promise me.""John, I promise. I…I…I promise. Whatever you need me to do, I'll do. I'll do my best in telling them. I don't know if they're going to believe me. They're probably going to think I'm crazy."

He said, "Tracie, they'll believe you. They just can't handle this right now. They can't handle me going to them. I need you to do this. They're in no position.

They can't handle it, so I need you to tell them this. They will understand. They will believe you. I know they will. Just do this for me."

"You got it. Absolutely you got it. You have my word I will pass it along."

And then he just said to me, "I'm out of time. I really gotta go. I'm really out of time. Tracie, I will be back. I promise you I'll be back to talk to you. My visits will be infrequent, but I promise you I'll be back." And he hugged me. "I'm outta time, and I gotta go, but before I go, real quick, I can't get over the turnout at my funeral. Amazing! I couldn't believe what I was seeing. I couldn't believe all the people. And certain people who were there, I couldn't believe it. Tracie, just trust me, this isn't the end. It's not the end, but I gotta go."

And . . . that's when I woke up. He was gone. It was so, so real. I could reach out and touch him. He was there. That grin! He put his arms out real wide and said, "This place is amazing! You can't fathom! I'm limited as to what I can say. I can see you, I can watch you. I'm fine!" He reiterated that message so many times.

Debbie sent me some pictures of her and John (photo 50 and 57, John and Debbie), and when I gave a seminar at the Edgar Cayce ARE Center in New York City in the summer of 2004, Debbie attended. I took a series of pictures of her. Some of them showed Debbie clearly (photo 51, Debbie), but one picture had a reasonably clear picture of John superimposed (photos 52–56, Debbie). If you take a close look at that image, you'll see that there's another face present as well. John's face is the larger, more prominent one taking up the lower left half (photo 55, Debbie), and the smaller face above and to the right (photo 56) resembles that of Edgar Cayce (photo 58, Edgar).[16] We all

---

[16] Lifetime photo of Edgar Cayce published with permission of Edgar Cayce Foundation.

had hoped that Edgar Cayce would make his presence known during the workshop, and we were delighted.

The most natural reaction to that picture by a discerning human mind is, "It's most likely faked. That collage of three faces could easily be created with a program like Adobe Photoshop, and there's no natural way for it simply to appear in a Polaroid picture."

That conclusion is true: (1) based on earthly knowledge, that picture is most likely faked, (2) it would be easy to create such a collage with modern computer techniques, and (3) there's no way by earthly physics for such an image of three living beings to show up superimposed over each other in a photograph in that way.

The catch is this: Based on spirit-world physics, that picture is possible, and I know for certain that it's a legitimate spirit picture. So do the six people in that New York City workshop who witnessed the untouched photo as it developed. It's one of many spectacular spirit photos we received that day.

I know from a decade of ITC research that such outstanding contacts are rarely random or spontaneous. They're almost always the result of intensive spirit-world planning and choreography. Our spirit group has to come close to our world in vibration, locate us in time and space, and then make the contacts happen—a very difficult feat, we are told. So among ITC researchers there is no end to the admiration, appreciation, and gratitude we feel toward our invisible colleagues, who make miracles happen in our work.

While I never met John Alberti, it is obvious to me that he was/is one of those people who knows instinctively how to get things done. He jumps into a situation and makes things happen. John and people like him will be valuable on both sides of the veil in the coming years, as we open ITC contact bridges around the world.

CHAPTER FIFTEEN

RECENT RESULTS AT THE MONROE INSTITUTE

In 2005, I spent two incredible weekends with advanced students at The Monroe Institute (TMI) near Charlottesville, Virginia, working with TMI Program Director Darlene Miller to facilitate three-day workshops with the luminator. The work of TMI involves Hemi-Sync techniques, which move the brain into altered states of consciousness in an effective, safe, and reliable way. With the help of special audio technology, TMI trainers help individuals to reach meditative states in a few days (in some cases a few minutes) that would ordinarily take months or years of advanced spiritual training to achieve. The technique was developed by Robert Monroe, founder of TMI, who once said, "The greatest illusion is that mankind has limitations."

We shattered that illusion over those two weekends, when we took many remarkable photos, including a striking image of the late Robert Monroe posing with his daughter Laurie.

The men and women I met at the two workshops ranged in age from the mid-thirties to mid-seventies. They reminisced matter-of-factly on personal experiences in parallel dimensions, paradise environments, alien cities, and future worlds—experiences that most people today would expect to hear about only in science fiction movies.

Laurie Monroe took over TMI after the death of her father, TMI founder Robert Monroe, in 1995, and she has been highly appraised by our spirit friends since then. That first became clear to me in 1997, when she and I were among a group of Americans researching spiritual sites in Brazil. During a healing session at a spiritist hospital, Laurie received an apport—an object that appeared out of thin air. A semi-precious green stone—a gift from our spirit friends—materialized on her stomach during the session, surprising the healer and the attending nurses.

I hoped to get a good picture of Robert with Laurie during the workshops, and the results exceeded expectations. He showed up at least twice. In the first photo (photo 59, Laurie), Laurie had the face of her father on the left (photo 61, Laurie), as well as an unidentified woman in profile (photo 60, Laurie). Isolating the left half of the face, I produced a composite face (photo 62, Laurie) that bears a good likeness to Robert Monroe (photo 63, Robert).

In another photo (photo 64, Laurie), Laurie showed up clearly, with no anomalies. In others (photos 65 and 66, Laurie), four distinct spirit faces appeared—Robert Monroe on the left (photo 67, Laurie), a woman in the middle (photo 68, Laurie), an unidentified woman on the right (photo 69, Laurie), and an unidentified man on the bottom (photo 70, Laurie). One of the female spirit faces, possibly the middle one (photo 68), could be Laurie's mother (photo 71, Laurie and Mary), shown in the picture with Laurie in 1959. There's not enough of that middle face showing to know for sure if it's Laurie's mom, but there is a trace of resemblance.

Jennifer took her first TMI Gateway course[17] in June 2005, after reading Robert Monroe's book, *Far Journeys,* which she says "popped off the shelf, as I understand Bob's books quite

[17] TMI's Gateway Voyage is a six-day program that fosters self-discovery, out-of-body experiences, and communication with and visits to other energy systems.

often tend to do." The course allowed Jennifer, for the first time in her life, to quiet her mind enough to go into a meditative state.

"I never thought I could be one of those people who meditate," Jennifer said. "Even after the training I didn't think I'd ever be able to quiet my mind without the Monroe frequencies and technologies. Now it's as though certain synapses have been activated in my brain so that I can go to those focus levels at will." During our afterlife-communication workshop that fall, we received some good spirit faces with Jennifer (photo 72, Jennifer), including that of a young man (photo 73, Jennifer). Jennifer didn't seem to mind the presence of the male spirit replacing her face in that picture (photo 73, Jennifer), but she said with a smile that she wasn't pleased by his big belly showing up on her body.

Basil had his introductory Gateway course at TMI in early 2002, after which he felt an increased spiritual sensitivity. A year and a half after the course he participated in a paranormal investigation aboard the Queen Mary, an ocean liner known to be haunted since being retired and docked permanently in Long Beach, California, as a hotel. One day the investigating team was gathered at the edge of the empty first-class swimming pool. As Basil stood with his back against the protective railing, he suddenly felt a presence behind him. There was a ten-foot drop into the pool, so it was physically impossible for someone to be standing behind him. He mentioned the presence to John, the team leader, who was standing in front of him.

John asked Basil if he could tell anything about the presence, or if it could speak.

Basil replied, "I don't know, let's try."

So John and the group began asking questions, which the spirit answered through Basil. The being said his name was Mr. Smith, but he had been misidentified on his death certificate as Mr. Brown. Apparently Smith and Brown had both been left on the doorstep of an orphanage in Liverpool, England. The authorities at the time had no idea who their mothers were, so the two infants were named Smith and Brown. The two boys became inseparable friends growing up. As a young man, Brown eventually moved to Chicago. Smith later boarded the Queen Mary to emigrate to America, meet up with his old friend Brown, and start a new life. While on board ship, Smith said he had had the fatal misfortune of falling from one deck to another, striking his head, and dying midway through the cruise. When the ship's purser wrote up the death certificate, he listed the deceased passenger incorrectly.

Basil explains that in those days a traveler's luggage had to have a tag that gave the name of the traveler on one side, and on the other side the name of his or her sponsor, or the person who would pay the immigrant's expenses upon arrival in America. Apparently, the purser read the wrong side of the tag on Smith's luggage.

Smith had been residing aboard the Queen Mary since his death, and now he was apparently delighted to have someone (Basil) with whom to speak. When Basil returned to his cabin after the incident at the pool, Smith followed him. Basil asked the spirit three times to leave the cabin, but when Smith left, he came right back a few minutes later. Basil says he wasn't frightened; he just didn't want to get in the habit of talking to spirits alone, as people overhearing him might think he was schizophrenic. Basil asked his spirit guides and guardians to take Smith out of the room, which they did, and the ghost remained out for the rest of the night.

The next morning Smith was standing behind Basil at the breakfast table. As Basil began to announce Smith's presence, a clairvoyant said at the same time, "Basil, I can see the fellow behind you."

Aware of Basil's discomfort with the tenacious ghost, the group did an experiment to try to bring Smith and Brown, both long dead, together. Hopefully that would allow Smith to detach from the earth and move home to paradise. With the ghost of Smith standing beside him, Basil again opened himself to serve as a medium. The team invited Brown to join them here on the Queen Mary. A few moments later, Basil saw the form of a man in spirit walking slowly toward them along one of the ship's corridors. When Smith recognized the man, the two spirits embraced like long-lost brothers. When Basil once again departed for his stateroom, Smith and Brown *both* followed him, and he grew concerned. He didn't want a spirit fan club developing around him. As it turned out, the two old friends were just escorting Basil as a sort of gesture of gratitude and farewell, for as soon as they reached Basil's cabin, they left for good.

Basil felt quite happy about that and, looking back on the experience, he believes that his English heritage helped to forge the connection with the two ghosts from Liverpool.

"I know that Gateway opened me up to this type of paranormal activity," Basil said, "even though it was more than a year since I'd taken the course." The incident on the Queen Mary was his first of that kind, but since then he has had many experiences in which spirits have spoken through him. "They're usually messages about love and enlightenment, or how to live a better life," he said. "[The messages] come from people on the other side who feel they have a story they want us on earth to know." Basil continued his connection with TMI, taking its Lifeline, Explorer 27, and Starlines courses. He attended my afterlife-communication workshop in October 2005, and had several anomalous photos taken.

The light anomaly shown in one photo (photo 74, Basil) is fairly common in the pictures taken in the presence of the luminator. When the machine is running, light from overhead fixtures often migrates down into camera range in a way that makes no sense in terms of worldly physics. However, in nonphysical realms, space and structure become more malleable. Also, realms are superimposed over each other, but they are not perfectly locked in place with each other. They seem to shift, largely as a result of thoughts and feelings of the beings in those realms. So when the luminator is running, and the physical and spiritual realms blend together, things that seem solid and stable begin to shift in ways that are imperceptible to the eye, but can be captured on film, especially in low-light conditions.

Another picture of Basil (photo 75, Basil) showed his face replaced by two half-faces of spirits, as shown in the composites (photos 76 and 77, Basil).

Keli (photo 78) is a flight attendant by profession and by nature a delightful woman who captivates people with her true-life stories and earthy descriptions. She frequently encounters people in spirit who are stuck near the earth, and she helps them move to the subtler paradise worlds. She has been especially busy after such disasters as 9/11 and the 2004 tsunami in southeast Asia. Keli is an author and popular guest on radio shows, where she shares highly personal psychic insights with listeners. On one occasion, the spirit of a beautiful, well-groomed sheltie hopped into the back seat of her car on the way to the studio, and Keli had a strong feeling that one of her call-in guests later that evening would know about that dog. Sure enough, a female caller asked about her dog who had recently died, and Keli described the dog who was now sitting at her feet there in the studio. The female caller let out a healing sob, and "the station manager freaked, as usual," said Keli.

In one picture we took during the afterlife-communication workshop, Keli's face was replaced by one that closely resembled a living relative (photo 79, Keli). When her family members later saw that picture, they immediately recognized the fellow, whom Keli prefers not to identify publicly. I know of other cases in which a face of a living person seems to appear in the Polaroid photo when that person is not present. Apparently their astral body is wandering away from the physical body.

Like Basil, Keli also had a photo with an impressive light anomaly, as well as a second face below and to the right of her face (photo 80, Keli).

Pete has died several times and been revived, and as a result has zero fear of death. He enjoys frequent spirit-world adventures, most of them spontaneous. These adventures are similar to what most people would call dreams, but much more vivid than the usual dream. During one of those out-of-body journeys he found himself in a government installation, where he encountered several men sitting in suits and ties, working at computer terminals. Startled by Pete's sudden appearance in their top-secret facility, they all stopped working and stared at him. Apparently they were working and existing at a subtler-than-physical level of existence, so Pete was visible to them. (Normally during his journeys he is invisible to others.)

He said that because of trips like this, he's firmly convinced that the U.S. government is involved in other-worldly research that is not made public. A colleague of Pete's once told him it's possible for a person to bring items, such as papers, back from out-of-body journeys, simply by cradling them in one's arms close to the chest, but Pete has never tried that.

Dee Jay and I were among those who shared a shuttle to the airport after the workshop, and she recalled a time several years earlier when she was on a precarious bus ride up a rough mountain road in Peru. During that trip, the careless bus driver had nearly driven off the road a couple of times. Dee Jay told me during our calm ride to the Charlottesville airport that she hadn't really been scared in Peru, thanks to her TMI training. "When it looked like we might all die, I just left my body," she said with a shrug. If the bus had wound up as a crumpled heap in a mountain ravine, Dee Jay probably would have gathered up the spirits of the other dead passengers and escorted them to paradise. I suspect that many TMI advanced students would take charge in a catastrophe in which they and others lost their lives. They'd know what to do, where to go, and how to get there.

George said he once entered a massive, museum-like building during his spirit-world travels, and in the lobby he passed by a large alien robot. It had bony facial features and visible ribs, and its body seemed to be composed of ceramics and metals. It was motionless, so George assumed it was just a statue. Inside the building he asked someone about it and was surprised to learn it was actually a living entity. He was told to ask the entity for an explanation, which he did on the way out. The entity said, "I'm glad you finally talked to me. I'm your guide." Since then George has had a close rapport with the being, whom he calls Bones. On one occasion Bones took George on a visit to an alien civilization with highly advanced structures and technologies that took his breath away.

(The pictures of Pete, Dee Jay, and George are not included in this book, but I thought their stories shed interesting light on the afterlife.)

Most of the pictures taken at the weekend workshops are being kept on file, in separate envelopes, at TMI and have not left the premises. The participants received copies. I received a CD with the images, which I'm using in this book.

PART FOUR

RESHAPING OUR LIVES
THROUGH SPIRITUAL INSIGHT

The luminator photos and other related images make up just a small piece of a massive, elaborate puzzle. The puzzle is embodied in the larger field of ITC research, especially the fascinating contacts received by the INIT group between 1995 and 2000. As the bigger picture comes together here, the significance of these smaller Polaroid pictures will become clearer.

Prepare to reflect on your mental model of reality and possibly feel it being stretched a bit.

CHAPTER SIXTEEN

KNOWING OUR HUMAN HERITAGE

For six years our INIT group received the most miraculous ITC contacts imaginable, complements of a cluster of ethereal beings who call themselves The Seven. They are the powerful forces who made it possible for our spirit friends to deliver poignant information through our technical equipment in the form of voices, images, and text. In various contacts throughout the 1990s our spirit friends reported on encounters with the ethereal beings, who make the decisions about what information will be sent to earth through ITC contacts. The ethereal beings met with our spirit team at the edge of the ethereal realm in a revolving round room with transparent walls. Shapes, lights, and colors of breathtaking beauty passed by outside, as music of the spheres played softly in the background. The ethereal beings seem to have unlimited goodness, wisdom, and power. When our spirit friends are in their presence they are overcome by indescribable bliss.

The ethereal beings provided some of their own life energies to open the ITC bridge between heaven and earth, so that from 1995 to 2000 we were able to get a taste of the miracles that will someday be possible through ITC research. We talked to our spirit friends on the telephone, we received long messages from them through radios, they sent us pictures of themselves and their world through TVs and computers, and they delivered detailed text messages—personal letters—to us through computers.

The Seven told us that they have accompanied our world for many thousands of years. That made me start to wonder: could they have showed up in some historical writings? While researching and writing this book I came to the conclusion that, yes, they inspired our ancestors to create legends of gods and spiritual beings that played an important part in many ancient cultures. The seven archangels of Judeo-Christian tradition, the four archangels of Islam, the Greek Titans and Olympians, the Roman pantheon and *numina* (formless divine entities), the Mesopotamian gods, and the Norse gods are some of the super-human beings of ancient legend who I suspect were patterned in part after The Seven, and perhaps other ethereal beings as well. Early cultures developed imaginative legends around the ethereal beings and often gave them rather bizarre human qual-ities. More recent civilizations during the past four thousand years gradually peeled away the legendary clutter and portrayed the ethereal beings in more realistic terms and concepts, but even today there are misconceptions. The Seven told us, for example, that they and other "angels" don't have wings. Our spirit friends added that The Seven are surrounded by auras and ribbons of rainbow light, and I suspect that early visionaries interpreted those light emanations as wings.

The Seven told us they came especially close to our world on six occasions, trying to help humanity to forge "a fruitful, endurable relationship with the light, ethereal realm of exis-tence." This, in a nutshell, is the story they told us. I've pieced it together from a series of reliable contacts from them, and I've filled in some holes with information from my subsequent research.

Long, long ago there was a large, beautiful planet circling our sun in an orbit between Mars and Jupiter. It was called

Marduk; it was also called Eden, and it was a paradise world inhabited by superhuman beings in a highly advanced civilization. The superhumans of Marduk had established colonies on nearby planets, including earth, where they studied the primitive hominids[18] native to this world. The massive technologies on Marduk got out of hand, resulting in an enormous explosion that blew the planet to bits and sent planetary shrapnel flying in all directions. Some of the debris rained down on the earth, ravaging life and sending the colonists scurrying for caves, where they sat out the climatic upheaval resulting from the asteroid impacts.

Eventually things settled down on earth, or Terra as they called this world, and the surviving superhuman colonists were now castaways there. Their highly refined bodies and minds were not suited to the rugged life on Terra, where entities killed each other for food, territory, and mating rights. For most of the colonists, this was a nightmare—a *terr*ible situation—but a few of the more adventurous superhumans apparently saw it as a rather *terr*ific opportunity for adventure (I emphasize these words because I suspect they emerged from our ancestor's powerful feelings about planet Terra). The brilliant and sensitive Edenites could not easily survive in such a ruthless and *terr*ifying world as earth, so they crossbred with the rugged natives, resulting in (1) mankind's proverbial fall from paradise and (2) you and me. We today are the products of crossbreeding between the god-like superhumans of Eden and the barbaric ape-men of earth. The destruction of Eden and the crossbreeding here on earth were the beginning of The Project, the purpose of which was and is to bring humanity back to God. We today are, simply, human, and we are part of The Project.

Stranded, our colonist ancestors and their descendants set about building a highly advanced civilization called Atlantis.

---

[18] Neanderthals? Australopithecus? I'm not sure at this time.

The king's capital was located in the North Atlantic where the island of Helgoland is today. Atlantis inherited many of the powerful technologies from the mother planet, which they used to pillage and destroy other civilizations in southern Europe. Terra was a violent world, and so the Atlanteans had evolved into a violent people. They sailed in fleets of ships with fierce animal heads built into the bows, striking fear into the hearts of people wherever they went.

Atlantis flourished in a war-like way until the technologies again got out of hand, and the Atlanteans destroyed their empire in a massive explosion that rocked the earth.[19]

Centuries after the destruction of Atlantis, a small civilization called Shanidar grew on the banks of the Euphrates River, some twenty-five miles south of present-day Baghdad in Iraq. Much of the knowledge and heritage of Atlantis and Eden were preserved in the Sothis Temple in Shanidar, where a circle of priests tried to figure out how to put some order into human cultures scattered around the world.

This was the first time after the fall of Atlantis that The Seven came close to our world. They came to help the lost and confused human beings, torn between two worlds, rise up from the pain and suffering of their murky existence. The Seven worked closely with the Sothis priests, feeding them knowledge and wisdom from the ethereal realm.

To the wretched human masses, the goings-on in the Sothis Temple must have seemed miraculous, magical, awesome, and down-right frightening. Shanidar thrived as an ancient city until the people became lazy and gave in to human weaknesses. Promiscuity, stealing, murder, and drug abuse prevailed, and the streets became overrun by the homeless. Eventually bar-

---

[19] We were not told the earthly timelines of all these events. Scientists whose minds aren't too boggled by all this information would be better able than I to piece together the events, based on known asteroid impacts, cave drawings, geologic upheavals in Europe, the advent of various hominid species, and so on.

barians tore down the city walls, killed the priests, and destroyed much of the ancient history stored in the Sothis Temple.

Just before that happened, the priests had their final meeting. As barbarians were tearing at the gates, the priests vowed to get together once again, in a future lifetime, in new incarnations, when voices could "speak from boxes" and when people could "move through light behind glass." At that future time they would try to resurrect The Project. Meanwhile, memories of Shanidar were buried in the sands of time.[20]

Centuries later the city of Babylon grew on the site where Shanidar had fallen. Around the eighteenth century BC, Babylon became the political center of the Euphrates Valley and capital of Mesopotamia. The Babylonians worshipped a god named Marduk, who might or might not have been one of The Seven. I suspect that The Seven made an important impact on the Babylonian culture, teaching them about humanity's extraterrestrial heritage, and the Babylonians created myths around the ethereal beings—myths that developed into the various gods with such names as Ea, Enlil, Marduk, and Nabu. The Babylonians gave those gods human qualities. Marduk is described in some ancient texts as a god who displayed a ruthless side, for example.

Like Shanidar, Babylon rose and fell.

Around 600 BC, Babylon had become a decadent civilization, looting other cultures, partying it up, and ignoring higher human ideals. In 528 BC, in the Babylonian palace, during a typical orgy, with wine flowing and the men enjoying their con-cubines, King Belshazzar was preparing to drink a toast to the riches he and his late father had looted. Suddenly a human hand materialized and, to the astonishment of everyone

---

[20] The story of Shanidar was conveyed by The Seven on March 3, 1998, through the computer of Maggy Harsch-Fishbach. Translated with permission by Hans Heckmann. Published in *Transdimension* (Jan–June 1991, vol. 1).

present, inscribed a message on the wall: *Mene, Mene, Tekel, Upharsin.* The king's knees began to shake, and he went pale. Those Aramaic words meant "count, count, weigh, and divide." No one in the room had a clue as to the underlying significance of the message, but the king had a feeling it wasn't good. The Hebrew sage Daniel was beckoned to the room, and he said it meant that the king's behavior has been weighed and found lacking, so his kingdom would soon be divided. That night the king was murdered.

Now consider an incredible event The Seven told us happened hundreds of years earlier in ancient Shanidar when it was in utter decay. People were homeless and dying in the streets, and substance abuse was rampant. The Seven reported to us in great detail the events going on in the Sothis Temple on that final day. The head priest, Alkbrat, addressed the other priests, and his message included the following:

> We have made a mistake in reaching an understanding with the pupils of Nephtos, because we believed that as the caste of scientists, they would help us convince the people that the Gateway to the Space-Time Bridge was the last hope for our sick world. But we have erred. They have measured, minced, and counted, and again, measured, minced, and counted, and could not recognize the true meaning of our search, because they could not recognize the truth that stood behind our endeavors—the inseparability of the spiritual from the material world— the opening of the door between these worlds.[21]

I think the message to the Babylonian king Belshazzar was facilitated by The Seven as an ancient form of ITC/automatic writing. They were trying to tell the king, "Look, you block-

[21] *Transdimension* (Jan–June 1991, vol. 1).

head, you've already counted, weighed, and divided your wealth over and over again. The world's in a terrible mess, and we've got lots to do, so get up off your lazy . . . ." I think they're giving us a similar message today by telling us in detail about the Shanidar civilization and allowing us to compare that ancient decadence with the decadence we see in today's world. Consider the following message from The Seven:

> Often we are not telling you anything new because our messages are common sense. However, they are meant to stimulate your desire to find out more about it. We do teach you things you cannot find in reference books. The purpose of our messages is to evoke in you efforts of recognition and discernment, without which humans cannot accomplish an "Ascent into Light." It is your task as INIT members to learn to understand the messages, to discuss them among yourselves, pass them on and explain them. This also makes the difference between your publications and those of others who delight to give their readers mainly the raisins and topping, but neglect the dough. Without raising their consciousness, humans will be unable to take the necessary steps to stop the decay of ethics and morals in your time. That will only happen when man understands what he is doing. And that shall have to be explained to him. It is your task as members of INIT to guide the readers through what is self-evident to you and make it understandable to them. You should guide them with patience and in an orderly fashion, so they can follow our thoughts. When you detect anything that is confusing, clarify it as much as possible. Sonia (Rinaldi) and Mark (Macy) are doing outstanding work in this regard. They

are capable of describing difficult things in a simple manner and to highlight it as needed.[22]

Today The Seven have again come close to our world to convey the same message that they have conveyed to humanity six previous times. We are once again at a critical juncture. We must get our lives in order, get our world in order, put a stop to the encroaching moral decay, and launch a project to forge a fruitful, endurable relationship with the light ethereal realm of existence, what they called "a gateway to the space-time bridge"—the completion of The Project. With modern technology, I believe that can be done more effectively today than ever before possible, at least since the time of Atlantis. I have high hopes for the future of our world, if we can see the light in the coming years.

We have also been told through ITC contacts that dark and troubled thinking in our world causes a loosening of the earth's crust and various forms of climatic instability. I have no doubt that a general housecleaning of our world—a reversal of the moral decay now underway—would alleviate and eventually eliminate the earthquakes, hurricanes, tsunamis, and other natural disasters ravaging our world with greater frequency. If we neglect to do the housecleaning ourselves in a controlled manner, then powerful forces will most likely sweep through our terrestrial home in the coming decades to clean house in a far more drastic way. That, I believe, is the message being conveyed to our world now, for the seventh time.

About those other four civilizations that rose and fell between the ancient time of Shanidar and Babylon and modern times—I think Persia might have been the third, as it was located in present-day Iran, not far from the site of Babylon and

---

[22] Excerpt of a contact by The Seven, received January 11, 1997, through the computer of Maggy Harsch-Fishbach. Translated with permission by Hans Heckmann. Published in *Contact!* (1997, issue 4).

Shanidar. And when King Belshazzar was murdered, Babylon was soon thereafter conquered by Persia.

Another chosen people might have been the Egyptians; seven was their most sacred number. Another might have been the Greeks, who communicated with the gods through their oracles. Or perhaps the Indians with their rich Hindu tradition of multiple deities, or the Chinese. I'm not sure at this time.

However, I believe that one of the most recent chosen people were the Hebrew Semites—or Jews—who spoke (I believe) to The Seven ethereal beings, not to God, through the Ark of the Covenant. The ark was a box about two feet wide, two feet high, and four feet long, which was kept in a sacred tent called the Holy of Holies. The ark contained Moses' clay tablets etched (again, by spiritual hands) with the Ten Commandments, and its cover was adorned with two golden cherubs. From a point midway between the cherubs, the voice of The Seven ethereal beings spoke directly to Moses or his brother, Aaron. I suspect that voice from the ark thousands of years ago sounded much like the contacts The Seven have made to us by phone and radio. Why do I believe that Moses and the others didn't speak directly to God? Because we were told by The Seven that no one speaks to God, not even ethereal beings. God is what they call the highest principle of life, the absolute reality. As The Seven told us in 1996, "As a limitless entity, the universe (God) can never be one of the creative individuals who are numerous in the cosmos."

I believe it was the hope and intention of The Seven, every time they came close to our world to work with us through the six chosen civilizations, to spread light, wisdom, and knowledge of God and spirit to humanity. That knowledge among humans would allow communication channels to open up. They met with only partial success, and so today they are approaching our world again, this time (I believe) with high hopes. Yes, they said, today is the seventh time they have come close to our world to accompany and guide us.

Who do you suppose the seventh chosen people will be? Let that question simmer in the back of your mind as you read on, and the answer will become clear as you reach the end of the book.

Hopefully it will also become clear what we today can begin to do to forge "a fruitful, endurable relationship with the light, ethereal realms of existence." It's not easy for us humans, with our mixed ape-god heritage and spread as we are all over this world, to forge an alliance with each other and with ethereal beings steeped in purity and light, but there are conditions in place today that could make such an alliance possible. That is the key to our future and to the fulfillment of the human heritage, the completion of The Project.

The members of INIT, for the most part, were not fully prepared for the depth and weight of this information that we received in the late 1990s. Our minds were boggled. None of us had a full grasp of The Project and the gateway to a space-time arch. The single exception was a woman who The Seven told us is an incarnation of one of the Shanidar priests involved in Project Sothis. While this book gives a flavor of the contacts received by INIT, their full meaning and implications will be given to the world, I hope, by that woman in the coming years, when she is ready to tell her story.

I suspect that she and other Shanidar priests in modern incarnations (we are told there have been several alive in recent decades), who are either growing old or already dead, will rise again in other incarnations in the coming years. I suspect they will continue to try to reunite in order to bring The Project to completion. There will be tremendous challenges (this is Planet Earth, after all), but the potential benefits for this world are unfathomable.

CHAPTER SEVENTEEN

A NETWORK OF GLOBAL VISIONARIES

Children and young adults today face the greatest opportunity for world peace in the history of our world. Modern technologies, especially the Internet and computers, make it possible for people all around the globe to talk to each other on a daily basis. There has never been a better chance to bring humanity together.

At the same time, young people today face the greatest challenges ever. The modern world has not only developed unprecedented technologies, but is also moving into a period of moral decay reminiscent of ancient Shanidar, Babylon, and the other great civilizations on the eve of destruction. Drug abuse is rampant, sex is a recreational pastime for unprecedented numbers of young people, violent crimes are widespread, and the wealthy enjoy conspicuous consumption while women and children starve to death in less-advantaged regions of the world.

In the coming years the world will need men and women who can commit to love and stability in their lives, their relationships, and their world. These visionaries will not succumb to the temptations of this world, and they'll reach out beyond political borders and religious ideologies to embrace each other in friendship, love, and goodwill.

Ethereal beings will see lights flickering in the darkness, and as goodwill spreads among the global visionaries, our world will begin to glow. Ethereal beings will come closer to our world, attracted to the lights, and these men and women of pure hearts will be chosen to forge a fruitful, endurable relationship between our world and the light, ethereal realms of existence. Communication channels to our world will open wide, as angels and departed loved ones call the visionaries on the phone, plant messages in their computers, show themselves on their TVs, and talk to them through their radios. Wisdom of the ages will stream into this world, raising us out of our present darkness.

Shanidar had its circle of priests who were in contact with The Seven; Babylonians had the Esagila complex containing a holy of holies where they communed with the god Marduk. The Egyptians had hundreds of gods grouped into families of seven, eight, or nine, and they called their hieroglyphic language *medu netcher,* or "words of the gods." The Greeks had their rich pantheon of gods (the Titans and Olympians), as well as their oracles—men and women who channeled messages from the gods. The Hebrews had their holy of holies containing the Ark of the Covenant, through which they spoke to high spiritual powers. Humanity in the future will have its ITC systems that are in touch with ethereal beings and supported by human and spiritual beings at various levels of existence. This system of communication between heaven and earth will allow wisdom and light to stream into our world through that network of global visionaries.

Judging from the experiences of INIT, I suspect the men and women in that network will probably face a rough road of accusations, insults, and envy, but if they can remain united in mutual trust and friendship, they will bestow on mankind some of the greatest gifts it has ever received. Meanwhile there's much to do on Planet Earth to restore moral order. If we can all become generally familiar with our animal side and our godly side—if we can come to know both our physical self and our spiritual self—then we can start making moral choices that will shape our lives, our communities, our nations, and our world in ways that will reverse the course of decay and stabilize the planet. We can give ourselves and our world, literally, new life.

The Seven gave us a definition of morals that I believe is completely new in our world: "to understand, to acknowledge, to devise, and to act." I thought about that statement for a long time, and eventually determined they must mean:

> **To understand** the information coming to us from ethereal sources through our higher selves, as well as (eventually) through well-established ITC systems,
>
> **To acknowledge** the reception of that information,
>
> **To devise** or modify that information so that it fits into our world situation, and
>
> **To act** on it—to put that knowledge to use in making this world a better place.

So there are things we can do in our personal lives to make things better in the community, in our nation, and in the world, to help restore moral order here on earth—a vital step toward the completion of The Project.

50. John and Debbie (p. 102)

51. Debbie (p. 102)

52. Debbie (p. 102)

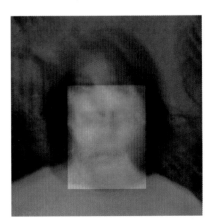

53. Debbie (p. 102)

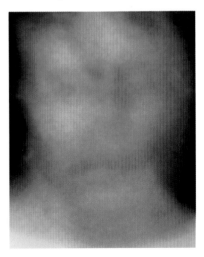

54. Debbie (p. 102)

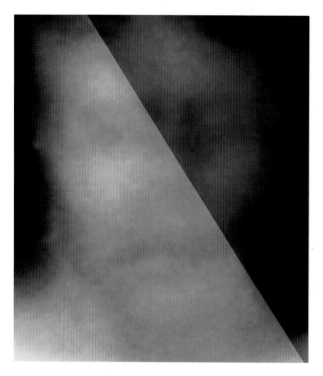

55. Debbie (p. 102)

57. Debbie and John (p. 102)

56. Debbie (p. 103)

58. Edgar (p. 102)

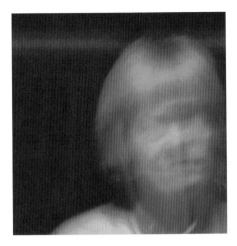

59. Laurie (p. 106)

60. Laurie (p. 106)

61. Laurie (p. 106)

62. Laurie (p. 106)

63. Robert (p. 106)

64. Laurie (p. 106)

65. Laurie (p. 106)

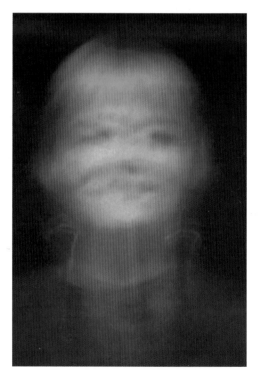

66. Laurie (p. 106)

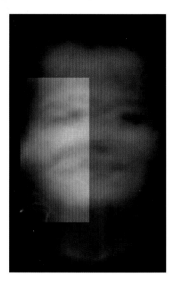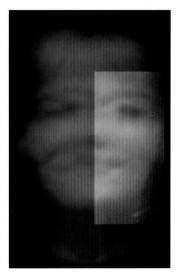

67. Laurie (p. 106)   68. Laurie (p. 106)   69. Laurie (p. 106)

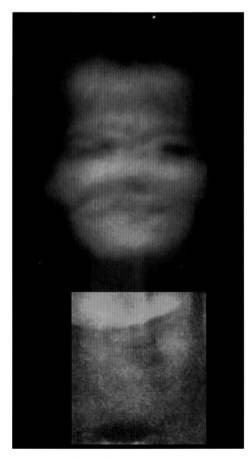

70. Laurie (p. 106)   71. Laurie and Mary (p. 106)

72. Jennifer (p. 107)

73. Jennifer (p. 107)

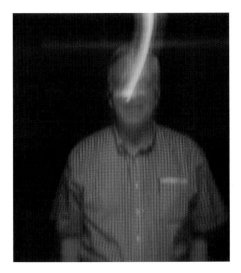

74. Basil (p. 109)

75. Basil (p. 110)

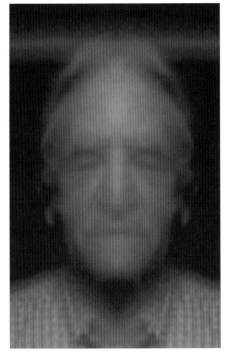

76. Basil (p. 110)

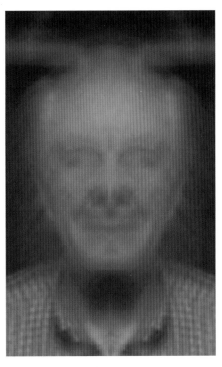

77. Basil (p. 110)

78. Keli (p. 110)

79. Keli (p. 110)

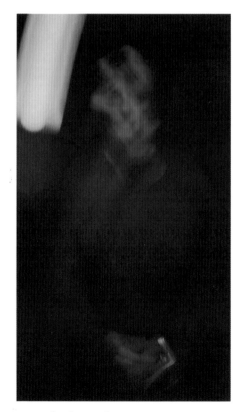

80. Keli (p. 110)

CHAPTER EIGHTEEN

CHARTING OUR PERSONAL DESTINY

More than two thousand years ago Rome was a vast empire, and the tribes and villages that were absorbed into it held onto many of their customs and beliefs because the empire tolerated diversity. One thing Rome insisted on, however, was taxation, because running an empire was expensive.

Among those smaller cultures taken in by the Roman Empire were the Hebrew Semites, or Jews. Jewish customs were strictly enforced by the Pharisees, self-righteous Jewish authorities who protected the purity of the Hebrew religion and begrudgingly complied with Roman demands. At one point the Pharisees were worried about the growing popularity of Jesus of Nazareth, a young Jewish miracle-maker who criticized both Hebrew tradition and Roman law, and who frequently told the crowds that the kingdom of God was far more important than worldly governments. The Pharisees tried to entrap Jesus by making him denounce the authority of Roman government, a crime punishable by death. They asked him, should taxes be paid to the government or to the church?

Jesus held up a coin and asked whose face was on it.

A Pharisee replied that it was the face of the Roman emperor, Caesar.

Jesus concluded, "Give to Caesar what is Caesar's, and to God what is God's."

The Pharisees were stymied. Jesus gave the only reply that could have ensured his freedom while maintaining the integrity of his commitment to God.

Jesus had a talent for boiling down complex ideas into easy-to-grasp parables and metaphors, which is one reason I love the guy. In this case Jesus said essentially that we are physical beings and spiritual beings at the same time, and we have certain obligations in each case. We should know what to give of ourselves physically and materially on one hand and what to give spiritually on the other hand. All of the world's great living religions share that view of human nature as a composite of the physical and spiritual self.

For me, this is the most important way to view human nature. It boils down all of the complex biological, medical, psychological, transpersonal, and esoteric ideas about human nature into a very basic model of the human being as a spiritual self and a physical self. Human nature then branches out into two main paths—the worldly and the spiritual—and each main path branches out into countless others. The worldly path goes into science, politics, economics, industry, and so on. The spiritual path branches out into the various religious and spiritual traditions. Through the path of science we can learn in as great a depth and detail as we wish about our physical-mental-emotional self. Through various spiritual paths we can get in touch with our spiritual self while exploring nonphysical realms, through practices such as prayer and meditation. But in my way of thinking, as long as we're alive on earth, regardless of which path we take, our search and our research should always lead back to that basic model. Otherwise we've lost our way. We must have unwavering knowledge that we are both physical and spiritual beings.

I know from my research over the past fifteen years, as well as from personal experience, that the physical self and spiritual self are like two opposing forces, trying to pull us in opposite directions, and part of our job on earth is to reconcile and integrate those forces. The physical self wants us to become totally engrossed in worldly things—time, space, gravity, money, sex, rich foods, fast cars, nice homes, and electronic gadgets. It worries about our earthly security, so it urges us to invest money wisely for our old age.

By contrast, our spiritual mind wants us to detach from all those worldly concerns, because when it's time to die and move on to the next world, all those attachments will hold us back. They'll make our spiritual vibration heavy so that we're unable to move too far from the earth. We could get stuck in the dismal realm for a while instead of moving on to paradise where we belong. Our spiritual mind has no interest in saving for the future. Money is to earth what life energy is to spirit—freely available everywhere. Simply use what we need when we need it, and give the rest away. More will come our way when we need it.

Our spiritual mind has our long-term interests at heart—our interests beyond this world—while the physical mind is caught up in short-term creature comforts and security in old age during this lifetime. One of the most important jobs we have during a lifetime on earth is to reconcile those two parts of our nature in order to come up with a healthy balance that works for us.

For me, maybe because I grew up in America, there were always plenty of ways to find physical and material gratification, but spiritual gratification was harder to find. If that's true for you, then there's a very simple, enjoyable heart meditation technique I've developed[23] to facilitate my spiritual refinement.

---

[23] Actually, mystics have been practicing various forms of heart meditation for centuries, and the Institute of Heart-Match in northern California has been studying the transformative effects of heart meditation for several decades.

I believe it's probably compatible with any religious or esoteric path, and it might work for you. Here's a short script:

> As we sit or lie in a comfortable position, we close our eyes, and relax our body. We locate our awareness, usually behind the eyes, and move it slowly to the back of the head, then down the spine to the heart. It's not like we're in the head thinking about the heart; it feels as though we have moved our thinking process into the chest. For centuries, mystics have called the heart "the seat of the soul." The soul is the real you and me, a piece of the Source, or God.
>
> Once we've moved to the heart, we pay attention to any unusual physical reactions—maybe a series of gentle jerks as the body feels surges of subtle energy, or maybe a loss of feeling in the hands and feet. Such reactions are normal as our body attunes to a more natural energy pattern. Now, from this point at the center of our being, we absorb all the light, love and wisdom that we can possibly absorb, from the source, from God. We feel our self, our soul, swell like a sponge. And as we swell with this divine light, we release it out into our spirit bodies and out further into our physical body. We let the light swirl through us, cleansing, purifying, and recharging us at every level.
>
> We pull more of this light from the source into our soul, and we let it out into our surroundings, transforming this room into a sacred space, a temple of love and light. Now, as we remain centered in the heart, we think of our loved ones on Earth and in spirit, and we feel the close heart connection. We send streams of love from our heart to theirs. Now, let's explore. . . .

Then we can continue to explore the wonders of spiritual reality silently in as personal and creative a manner as we wish, until we decide to come back to our conscious, waking, in-the-head state.

Shortly after discovering the effects of this meditation, I recited it slowly into a tape recorder as a guided visualization, leaving ten or twenty seconds of silence between sentences. I also added some nice, soothing music. You're welcome to do that too. Or you might want to get a copy of the *Bridge to Paradise* CD,[24] which contains Hemi-Sync tones to facilitate entering a meditative state. Doing this exercise several times a week, especially when using the *Bridge to Paradise* CD, can greatly accelerate our spiritual development. Practices such as this can help us, while we're still on earth, to prepare for our final journey to paradise by raising our spiritual vibration.

There are many ways to develop our spiritual side. Some people find an accomplished teacher from whom to learn proven techniques, such as meditation. Others prefer to find their own path. Some people like to join a religious or spiritual group, and still others seem to be pulled onto a spiritual path by other-worldly forces, sometimes during their dreams and daydreams, or during near-death experiences (NDEs) and out-of-body experiences (OBEs).

Meditation is arguably the most effective, time-proven method of achieving spiritual enlightenment here on earth. When meditation is new to us, stilling the mind can be a challenge, and a teacher can be helpful. The Hindu culture in India for centuries has been rich with men and women who mastered the art of meditation and became teachers for others. One of those masters was Paramahansa Yogananda, who moved to America in 1920, at a time when eastern mysticism was virtually unknown in the west. To illustrate the challenge of meditation, Yogananda reflected on an incident early in his training when he had had difficulties quieting his mind. One day his teacher could sense the boy's frustration and called him to his side. Yogananda was at first annoyed by the interruption, then

---

[24] I've produced this CD in collaboration with Monroe Products of Lovingston, Virginia. Listeners are guided through a heart meditation, then on to a journey to paradise with the Monroe Institute's Hemi-Sync sounds in the background.

embarrassed when he realized his teacher was fully aware of his cluttered thoughts.

The teacher reached out and rapped him softly with a fist above the heart. Yogananda's body froze in place, the air was pulled from his lungs, and his mind and spirit streamed out of his body like light. His body felt thick and dead even though he himself felt more alive than ever before. He could see in all directions, and the very ground became a semi-opaque substance through which he could see sap and fluids moving through the roots of trees. As his spirit became finer and finer, the world around him began to vibrate at a pace that became agitated, then violent, until everything suddenly melted away into a sparkling ocean of bliss. He felt himself merging with the countryside, then all of India, then the earth, stars, and galaxies—everything. The light of the universe became dense and heavy as a more powerful and at the same time far more subtle light streamed all around him, emitted by an eternal source, creating trillions of universes in all their glory. It all would have been an overwhelming experience if Yogananda hadn't realized intimately that the eternal source was in his heart. At the very center of his being, he *was* that infinitely creative source.

Then, suddenly, his unbounded consciousness was pulled back into his body, and his lungs filled with air in a huge gasp. After tasting immortality, his body felt like a dense, heavy prison, and he wished he could leave it behind. His teacher smiled and told Yogananda there was still much on earth he had to do, but in time he would once again, forever, be one with all.[25]

Another young man in the Far East named Siddhartha sought wisdom and knowledge from many wise men, but no one had the answers he was seeking. So he decided to find his

---

[25] Adapted from *Autobiography of a Yogi, Paramahansa Yogananda* (Los Angeles: Self-Realization Fellowship Publishers, 1946).

own way to spiritual enlightenment by detaching from worldly things. After several years of marriage to a beautiful woman, Siddhartha entered a six-year period of austerity and severe fasting. After becoming little more than skin and bone and very weak, he was still enmeshed in this world; he decided that a strong body would be necessary for his quest, and he began to eat and regain his strength.

Once he was strong again, he retreated to a forest to continue his search for truth. He sat under a Bodhi tree day after day—by some accounts, for several weeks—determined not to leave until either he became enlightened or until his blood would run dry. During his meditations he was visited by various spirit entities, ranging from the most beautiful and alluring to the most hideous and fearsome he could imagine. These visions were *maya,* or illusions meant to distract him from his path.

Siddhartha continued to explore within, moving ever closer to that central source of total knowledge, until finally, in the summer of his thirty-fifth year, he achieved enlightenment. Every shred of ignorance was washed away, and a deep inner knowledge of the universe filled his mind. As he entered this state of *nirvana,* Siddhartha became known as the Buddha, and he developed an eight-fold path around Four Noble Truths, which might help others to enlightenment.

In the Middle East, the Prophet Mohammed was pulled onto a spiritual path during a vivid dream, OBE, or NDE. He had a vision, or *Mir'aj* (an Arabic term that evolved into the English term *mirage,* or illusion), in which he ascended in vibration to visit the seven heavens—the astral and ethereal realms—accompanied by two of the archangels (at that time called Gabriel and Michael). Along the way he encountered the spirits of Adam, John the Baptist, Jesus, Joseph, Enoch, Aaron, Moses, and Abraham.

When Mohammed reached God, or Allah, the Source, he was given fifty prayers to bring back to earth. Anyone reciting those prayers daily would be in good grace with Allah. But on his way back to earth he was intercepted by Moses, who urged him to return to the seventh heaven to whittle down the prayer list. Mohammed took the advice and eventually came away with five daily prayers that would keep him and his followers close to Allah in their thoughts, words, and actions. He brought the five prayers back through the paradise of the astral realm and through the torments residing in the dismal realm before returning to his bed in Mecca. The five prayers became a cornerstone of every Muslim's life.

Those are techniques used by some of the world's greatest teachers when they themselves were searching for spiritual advancement—learning from a teacher, finding one's own path, and following inner guidance and inspiration. Today we on earth have the choice to follow the path of Buddha, Mohammed, Christ, or some of the other great spiritual masters and prophets, or we can forge our own path based on our spiritual understanding. Regardless of which path we choose, spiritual pursuit is rarely easy, as it involves coming to terms with our addictions and compulsions, and with the many worldly temptations that stimulate our animal side and repress our godly side. But once we accept that path, the rewards are boundless.

In my own search over the years, I've found that if there is any one thing on earth that is close to a ticket to paradise—something we can do while alive on earth to ensure a happy afterlife—it is this prayer spoken daily:

> Dear God, purify my thoughts, words, and actions. Purify my thoughts, words, and actions. I ask my ethereal guides to help me spread your love, light, and wisdom in this world through my thoughts, my words, and my actions.

Praying can actually lower our spiritual vibration if it is consistently self-serving or driven by false piety, but this particular prayer strips away all those obstacles and helps us to commit to working directly with God, helping God to fulfill God's plan with the help of powerful beings from the ethereal realm. We say the prayer daily, not as a set of empty words to get to heaven, but as an earnest commitment to be God's servant. As we assimilate the prayer into our lives, powerful forces mobilize—sometimes very quickly, sometimes gradually—to help us become instruments of God's will. Motivation is important.

MODERN ISSUES AND THEIR SPIRITUAL IMPLICATIONS

These issues often come up during question-and-answer periods when I give ITC seminars and workshops, so they apparently are on people's minds today.

Suicide. If we commit suicide in midlife, we might remain earthbound, hanging around the earth as a lost soul for awhile[26] in confusion. When we finally get to paradise we'll feel a twinge of regret. We'll think, "I couldn't wait ten more minutes (say, thirty years of earth time)? What a wasted opportunity." Our guides will concur: "What a waste!" Suicide is not a way to escape emotional problems or addictions, which accompany us into the next life and are often much more difficult to overcome without a physical body.

While the problems of being earthbound for several decades, or even for several centuries, might seem rather small and insignificant from the viewpoint of a spirit for whom time passes quickly, they can cause a lot of grief for those of us trying to lead a meaningful life here on earth. Earthbound spirits often move into living human bodies as spiritual parasites, and their

---

[26] "Awhile" might be several years or decades or centuries, since three years on earth pass like a minute in the dismal realm. That's not intended as an equation (1 minute = 3 years), but as a general statement of the notable time differential between earth life and spirit life.

moods, attitudes, and compulsions rub off onto the human hosts. Since most earthbound spirits are confused and troubled, and many are malevolent or addicted to drugs, they often create turmoil in human lives, families, and other social groups. Life on this rugged planet is difficult enough for ape-gods like us without the extra burden of neurotic and psychotic invisibles sharing their troubles with us indiscriminately.

Ideally, all earthbound spirits would move to the finer, happier spirit worlds where they belong, but they get stuck here by the lower vibrations produced by their troubled thinking. There are many beings on both sides of the veil working hard to move lost souls to paradise, but since earthbound spirits are engrossed in the earth, they usually don't notice the presence of spirit guides and helpers. So the guides wait patiently in some cases, and in others they drop in from time to time to see if the lost soul is ready to go home yet.

The power of prayer is tremendous. Prayers generated on earth can generate big changes in the dismal realm. Praying for lost souls can send streams of light and love into their dark, confusing world, so that they can actually see the spirit guides who would otherwise be invisible to them.

Assisted suicide. When a patient is dying of a degenerative disease, assisted suicide has no harmful effects on the afterlife scenario, as long as the patient has found emotional peace in life and in relationships with others. If the person is well versed in spiritual reality and comfortable with his or her fate, but enduring terrible pain, assisting the end of life carries no harmful spiritual consequences for anyone. (Legal consequences? Maybe. That's why it's always good to discern between "what is Caesar's and what is God's.")

But very often assisted suicide is not necessary. If a dying person is at peace with his or her spiritual nature and the paradise that awaits, the death process often proceeds quickly and smoothly. Fear and uncertainty about the afterlife—a desperate craving to stay attached to the physical world—can prolong the dying process.

Abortion. Our spirit friends have told ITC researchers that when a person in the astral world plans to incarnate, he or she sometimes enters a healing tank in the astral realm to grow younger and younger, through infancy, into a spiritual cell. The spiritual cell enters the woman on earth around the time of fertilization of her physical egg, and that cell follows the growth of the egg. As the egg grows into an infant, the spirit cell develops into a package of spirit bodies connected to the physical body by the proverbial silver cord.

If the egg or young fetus is aborted prematurely, the person in spirit returns immediately to the astral world. Our spirit team asked one of these aborted spirits about the experience. He said that he had received such a small taste of physical living that the entire experience was quickly forgotten and of no consequence whatsoever. There is no reason for the would-have-been mother to harbor any guilt over the fate of her fetus's spirit.

This description is not intended as a license to have an abortion; it's simply what we were told through ITC systems. I feel that abortions shouldn't be used routinely as a birth control method, but if for any responsible reason a pregnant woman chooses not to bear a child, an abortion will do no spiritual harm to anyone. Guilt or remorse on the part of the mother, hostility on the part of anti-abortionists, and other such destructive emotions will always lower the spiritual vibration of the person harboring those emotions, but the abortion itself has no spiritual consequences.

Cryogenics and life support. Death is a natural *coup de grace* of our earthly lives. Postponing death through artificial means can cause problems for the spiritual self. The spirit of a comatose patient, for example, remains in a confused state, trapped between heaven and earth, especially when the coma is prolonged with life-support systems. The spirit can't move into the next world until the physical body dies, and it cannot play a useful role in this life on earth with a nonfunctioning body. There comes a time to release comatose patients to a better life by removing life support.

Cryogenics traps the spirit in the same frustrating state. We were told of a famous man (whom I'll call W) who chose to have his body frozen at the moment of death. Our spirit friends tell us that W's spirit is in a confused state at the moment, stuck between the spirit world and earth, and will remain that way until his body is allowed to die.

Organ transplants. Transplants, especially heart transplants, can cause a bit of confusion if the donor has no understanding of the afterlife. When the donor's spirit leaves its body, it might remain attached to the living organ for a while and move right in to the body of the organ recipient. (A colleague of mine believes that aspects of the spirit might be left in the cells of the organ, but I don't know about that.) As the organ recipient recovers, he or she will discover many moods and preferences and prejudices characteristic of the donor.

Ideally, organ donors would have been spiritually educated before they died so they'd know when it's time to detach from the earth and move on to paradise. In any case, prayers here on earth during and after the transplant surgery can help the donor's spirit find its way home to paradise, with the help of spirit guides and intercessors.

Capital punishment. Execution of a violent criminal usually releases a troubled spirit from a troubled body. That spirit often stays close to the earth and gets surreptitiously involved with one or more living individuals. It moves into people's auras and sometimes stays there indefinitely. The spirit of the criminal shares its troubles with the living person, who takes on some of the attitudes and compulsions of the spirit. Otherwise good and decent (but sensitive and perhaps emotionally unstable) individuals become unsuspecting hosts to the spirit. In this way, capital punishment creates more criminal behavior, recycling the problems back into the human population.

It would be much better if the convict were emotionally rehabilitated and spiritually educated before dying, and the spirit moved away from earth to a finer vibration after death.

We on earth can protect ourselves from such spiritual parasites by harboring an attitude of love and joy, by remaining emotionally stable, and by avoiding drugs and alcohol that open us to negative spiritual influences. But a more comprehensive solution will involve educating society about the existence of troubled spirit worlds and instituting projects to clear away the darkness from around our planet.

In the future I believe many people will be trained to assist in rescue work—moving trapped souls to paradise with the help of spirit guides. Everyone from a young age will be taught effective methods of protecting oneself spiritually. Spiritually minded people will work together to protect people within their communities, especially the children. Meanwhile, capital punishment today could be replaced with diligent efforts to cleanse criminals spiritually.

⌖

During our lives on earth it's never too late to begin housecleaning—to commit to the thoughts, words, and actions that raise our spiritual vibration to the paradise level. Whether we choose to do that through the teachings of time-proven religions or through secular practices of morals and ethics, those changes can have a profound effect on our afterlife experiences. Choose a path that best resonates with you. Follow it to build inner strength, to overcome addictions, and to shake off unhealthy spiritual influences. The baggage that we gather in this lifetime includes:

- Our addictions;
- Our preoccupation with time, space, sex, food, and other earthly realities;

- Our fears, suspicions, resentments, lust, and other troubled emotions that served our ancestors well in escaping predators, protecting territory, mating and surviving, but have no place in paradise.

The more baggage we can shed, the finer our spiritual vibration becomes, and the higher we can ascend into paradise after we die.

It's almost impossible to get rid of all of that baggage, so we'll invariably carry some of it with us to the other side, and that's no cause for alarm. But the more we work at it now, the more loving and supportive spiritual influences will move into our life to help us. There are many forces on the other side poised to move in and help people on Earth. As our ethereal friends told us:

Children of Terra! When we come to take you home at the end of your lives, we sometimes find you in great haste, dashing around, trying to find order in your spirit and heart. It's as though you have guests coming in a few minutes, and you're hiding things under the furniture and sweeping dust under the carpet because you feel you neglected them and you're now ashamed. Relax, dear people! We come only to greet you, not to judge you. Your lifetime is like an hour of testing, so how can we judge you before the entire period of learning is complete? You try to imitate us because your religions tell you to, which is nice, but don't overdo it. As you say, you're only human, so don't be too hard on yourselves. You're not perfect, but that's no reason for us to find you repulsive or to be condescending.

We are with you when you're lonely and grieving, we lie beside you when you're sick, and we ease your burden when you're suffering. We love humans, but you sometimes expect this love to give you things we cannot give because you are not prepared to receive them. We recognize that your desperation, skepticism, doubt, and anger are just baggage you accumulate during your journey, but rest assured, once you return to us you'll feel like the child sitting happy and securely on its mother's lap. At your time of transition, don't make things hard for yourself and each other. Lighten your hearts and remove your masks in front of each other, and you'll be ready for paradise when we come to take you home.[27]

Between 1995 and 2000, my colleagues and I received many important contacts from The Seven. While researching for this book, I've come to believe that they are the seven archangels who have followed humanity for tens of thousands of years, offering protection and guidance for our development. In recent years they have been providing direction for the ITC project unfolding in the world. At the time of this writing, the communications are dormant, as the information already sent spreads around the world and consolidates into the human psyche. When conditions are right, the contacts will resume. That might be five months or fifty years from now. It will depend largely upon how quickly spiritual understanding and the possibilities of spirit communication are embraced by mankind. How quickly, in the face of spiritual reality, can we evolve from a spook-show mentality to a genuine appreciation of miracles? When will fear be replaced by awe when we think about death and the afterlife? Answers to those questions will largely determine the fate of ITC research, and the outcome of The Project.

---

[27] Excerpt of a contact by The Seven, received October 14, 1995, through the computer of Maggy Harsch-Fishbach. Translated with permission by Hans Heckmann. This was one of the first in a series of miraculous contacts that we received from The Seven after the formation of INIT in September 1995, and I published it at the top of the first page of the first issue of *Contact!* (1996, issue 1).

CHAPTER NINETEEN

CHARTING OUR GLOBAL DESTINY

I like to keep things as simple and clear as I can, reducing complex ideas to basic models. That includes ideas about world affairs, a subject I was immersed in before developing cancer and going through my spiritual transformation. Macro issues and world affairs might at first seem out of place in a book about spirituality, which is a very personal issue. But I'll explain how these things fit together and how the pictures I get in the presence of the luminator fit into the larger picture of life on earth.

I see today's studies of economic, political, and social systems as cumbersome and unwieldy. I believe they would be stabilized if they rested on a simplified, basic model that gave them order and direction and fostered compatibility among different viewpoints. I'm convinced that a model such as the following two-part one is crucial to charting our global destiny.

PART 1: SOCIAL-POLITICAL SYSTEMS

The basic building blocks of social systems are people and products, just as the basic building blocks of biosystems (human bodies, trees, insects, fishes, etc.) are body cells and molecules. People in society, like cells in a body, are the basic living units that give the system substance and life. People and their social groups (families, clubs, communities, businesses, for example) use products such as buildings, cars, and highways the way that cells and organs use such molecules as hormones, enzymes, proteins, and nucleic acid —to provide structure and energy for the system's inner workings, including transportation, maintenance, energy production, and regulation.

Obviously there are differences between social systems and biosystems. First, cells in the body are selfless entities, dedicated to their roles, which makes regulation of a biosystem highly efficient. People in society, on the other hand, enjoy liberty and the pursuit of happiness; as a result, regulating a social system is much more difficult, and many mistakes are made.

A second difference is that most biosystems simply live in an environment and extract what they need in terms of food. If the environment doesn't have what a biosystem needs for survival, the biosystem either moves on to another environment or dies. Social systems, on the other hand, have to take on the role of environmental caretaker as well as being a consumer of resources. Again, that makes the regulation of a social system more difficult, and there's a greater chance for mistakes to occur.

People fit into families, clubs, churches, communities, businesses, and other social groups within the social system in the way that cells fit into body organs and tissues. But people are versatile and need variety, whereas specialized body cells thrive on routine. Pure communism makes the mistake of overlooking people's need for diversity and inspiration, patterning the social system more closely to a biosystem and likening roles of individuals to the roles of body cells. The result is loss of will and a broken spirit. Capitalist democracy, on the other hand, glorifies the diversity and needs of individuals and special interest groups, often neglecting the social system's overall needs for stability over time. The result is an inability for long-term planning and unpredictable policies from one presidential administration to the next. Social systems in the future need to find that critical balance between the need of individuals to be free and the need of the social system to be stable.

There are overlapping levels within all social systems. Individuals make up families, clubs, churches, communities, and businesses, and these groups fit into states, provinces, industries, transnational corporations, religious sects, ,and other large organizations, which in turn fit into nations and religions and multinational alliances, which in turn make up the society of mankind. So how is all of this activity at all these levels regulated? Not very well, actually. Many people and many social systems are constantly vying for power, trying to run the show. The ape-side of our nature has always been about the struggle to prevail, and it boils over into our social systems.

Knowing what we know about our physical nature (our ape-side) and our spiritual nature (our god-side), perhaps in the future we can activate our godly side more fully, then employ a simple formula for regulating social systems. The formula is this: Decisions are always made at the lowest level, but high enough to take into account the needs and interests of everyone and every group that will be impacted by the decision.[28]

I think that's probably how regulation occurs within a biosystem, and it would work well in social systems. It just makes good sense to distribute the decisions throughout the system, letting each decision be made at the lowest reasonable level.

In the future, ideally, more and more people will make an effort to develop spiritually, their values and attitudes will diffuse into social groups, and responsible regulation will occur at all levels, from individual (human rights) to global (a strong, well-run, well-respected United Nations).

---

[28] Dutch economist Jan Tinbergen shared that idea—of decision-making at the lowest possible level—with me as I was assembling my book *Solutions for a Troubled World* in the 1980s.

A system of people and products (a social system) is like a system of cells and molecules (a biosystem) in that it has structural and energy needs that have to be satisfied by what it consumes. A social system consumes resources in the way a biosystem consumes food.

That ratio between a system's needs and its resources is the basis, or foundation, of economics:

$$\text{Economic health} = \frac{\text{Natural resources}}{\text{System needs}}$$

According to this model, all of the other complex measurements of modern economics would be reassessed in relation to that ratio.

Ideally, the basic aim of a current and future social system is to minimize its structural and energy needs while finding adequate, appropriate resources to satisfy those needs. Minimizing needs can be accomplished with planning and foresight by such methods as reducing the population (for example, family planning), reducing per-capita consumption (for example, recycling and moderation), and developing innovative techniques and technologies that require less energy and fewer building materials to achieve equal or better results. Resource supplies can be increased by such means as acquiring more territory (rarely a wise plan in a world of 191 tightly consolidated nations), opening untapped resource fields (as long as environmental considerations are responsibly made), foreign trade, and innovations leading to new forms of resources.

A social system that ignores or resists policies to minimize needs will invariably feel the consequences when those needs go out of control. Those consequences range in severity from inflation and recession, to economic collapse, genocide, and famine. It's important that social systems develop sound policies to minimize their structural and energy needs before their economies fly out of control.

Modern capitalism is based on the outmoded idea that the economy is healthy only when it's growing—when needs are increasing and more resources are found to satisfy those needs. That idea worked well in America during two hundred years of abundance, when small communities of European immigrants found a vast land of seemingly endless resources before them, but it works no longer. Traditional capitalism can only lead to destruction and war in a future world of burgeoning needs and dwindling resources, as desperation compels capitalist nations to acquire resources militarily. To avoid a future of continuing chaos and destruction, there will have to be a new focus on minimizing needs through sensible planning.

❧

Even if the model outlined above is a right and proper view of the true nature of humanity (as I believe it is), it won't automatically solve the problems of this world unless one additional factor is added to the mix: Humanity will have to find a way to foster the god-side of individual human beings while putting the ape-side of human nature in its place. We'll have to find effective ways to bring love, trust, and joy into the forefront of human affairs, starting at the personal level and spreading out into all of the social systems. That process will gradually wash away the fears, doubts, resentments, and lusty urges that play such a big role in human lives today, stirring up conflicts at all levels of society.

It could be argued that if we brought out humanity's god-side and washed away the ape-side, then *any* social, political, economic, or religious system would work fine, and they'd all work fine together, and the world would be a peaceful place. I'm not so sure of that. Nearly all of today's political, economic, and religious systems have built-in creeds or dogmas or ideologies that stir up troubles. They encourage exclusivity, discrimination, suspicion, a sense of superiority, conspicuous consumption, callousness to the suffering masses, and much more. I believe that a neutral model, such as the one introduced above, will be needed to gradually wash away the incompatibilities that allow those dark aspects to grow. And that will make it easier for humanity's god-side to prevail.

Meanwhile, how do ITC contacts in general, and the luminator images in particular, fit into this big picture? Bringing the god-side of human nature into human affairs will require a spiritual awakening. Most people in today's world haven't an inkling of what really happens to us after we die. Many people don't even believe in the afterlife. Before there can be a global awakening to the human spirit, people everywhere will have to be convinced that life goes on after they die, and the luminator images can help to convince people of that. They also provide solid evidence—veritable proof—that nonphysical beings (spirits) interact with our world.

Once humanity accepts its spiritual nature and makes an effort to commit to that aspect of itself, then the earth will be fertile for the more elaborate ITC bridges to open up. The Seven ethereal beings told us that ITC cannot come to this world in its full glory until there is a psychospiritual readiness prevalent on the planet. If ITC bridges were opened up in today's world, the fears and resentments that exist among nations, religions, and individuals would quickly corrupt those bridges. The contact field would become impenetrable by the finer spirit beings, and negative spirit groups would move in and use the existing bridges to convey messages of malice into our world, further destabilizing human affairs.

So, the destiny of our world, as I see it, is:

1. To adopt some sort of simplified, reasonable model of world affairs from which all social, political, and economic systems can evolve compatibly.

2. Meanwhile, let humanity awaken spiritually as people everywhere become convinced of their spiritual nature and comfortable with the thought of an afterlife. (The luminator images can help in that regard.)
3. Forge fruitful, endurable relations with the light, ethereal realms of existence. (This will be achieved when ITC bridges open up around the world, made possible by the global awakening.)

Meanwhile, the luminator probably has potential for many disciplines today, especially psychiatry. For years I've believed that schizophrenia, psychosis, multiple personality disorder, Tourette's syndrome, and many other maladies have spiritual causes as well as the recognized, well-accepted genetic and environmental causes. Troubled spirits stuck near the earth attach themselves to people in a parasitic relationship instead of moving on to the worlds where they belong. Their troubled moods rub off on the human hosts, producing various forms of antisocial behavior. Using luminator images, perhaps therapists could determine the degree to which spirit attachment is a factor in a patient's illness. Eventually they might find that certain spirits cause certain neurological, chemical, and behavioral changes in the client, or certain conditions in the client attract certain troubled spirits.

In the future I believe that the most effective treatments for most mental illnesses will include spiritual understanding coupled with techniques of personal spiritual protection and a loving attitude free of fear, resentment, and other troubles that attract destructive spiritual influences. These spiritual treatments will be applied in addition to psychiatric therapies currently in use. I believe that coming to terms with hormones, addictions, egos, and other physical-world obstacles prepare us for the right spiritual attunement, and doing that, I believe, will eliminate most mental illnesses from our world.

For now, highly effective pharmaceutical drugs can close down the subtle senses that open human minds up to troubled spirits. Drugs such as Seroquel, prescribed by psychiatrists, can strengthen the protective cloak that blocks spiritual access to vulnerable minds. They can be extremely effective in emergency situations, such as severe mood disorders and psychotic breaks induced by alcohol or recreational drugs.

When those pharmaceutical drugs are applied in the future, hopefully patients can then begin to explore paths of spiritual development. They can be freed of any recreational-drug or alcohol addictions and destructive thought processes that break down psychospiritual coherence and allow troubled spirits to move in. Patients can then replace those chemical addictions and self-destructive thought patterns with spiritual practices that are much more gratifying in the long run. Through spiritual practice, people learn to anchor themselves in love, awe, trust, and happiness, so that when the protective cloak between mind and spirit is gently brought down (for example, through meditative practices and prayer), people are connected to brilliant, beautiful, and powerful spiritual influences from the finer worlds of existence—paradise and beyond.

CHAPTER TWENTY

KNOWING YOUR PERSONAL MISSION
FOR THIS LIFE AND BEYOND

My mom used to tell me, "Mark, you really pack a lot of information into your words." She let me know early in life that I
had a flare for writing. Also for music. I could very easily have
become a musician instead of a writer. In fact, when I see a movie
or documentary film about rock stars of the '60s and '70s, I feel
an emotional yearning well up inside of me, as though a part of
me wanted to pursue that purpose in this life—to have written
songs and played in a band during those tempestuous times.
But another part of me won out—maybe a part that wanted to
protect me from my own susceptibility to drugs.

For whatever reason, I fired up my writing skills and let my
musical ear simmer. Over the years I've developed my skill for
figuring out complex subjects and expressing them clearly in
simple terms. Most of my life I knew that when I relaxed and
daydreamed or meditated, my five physical senses would close
down, some higher sense would open up, and my mind was fed
important insights. I'd regain enough conscious awareness to
capture the ideas on paper or on audiotape to be transcribed later
on. Then I'd digest and process the information to understand its
significance and how to fit it into my life and my writing.

Now, thanks to ITC research, I know that daydreaming and meditation opened me up spiritually so that bright spiritual minds beyond this world could feed ideas and concepts to me, through my own higher self.

I'm sure that the greatest songwriters and composers—from Bach and Debussy to Gershwin and Mancini, to Dylan and Lennon-McCartney—all received direct inspiration from bright spiritual minds. They channeled their music at times when their minds were quiet and reflective. Likewise with brilliant artists, architects, surgeons, chefs, authors, screenwriters, and other creative people; they are guided by bright spiritual minds beyond this world.

There are also dark and troubled spirit minds on the other side, feeding information to the minds of swindlers, thieves, modern-day pharisees, ghouls, and murderers. The dark spirit minds also like to support writers and others who influence the public, planting in their minds horror scenarios and feelings of hatred that show up in novels, songs, and other creative works. It's up to these creative men and women to be discerning about the types of spiritual influences they allow in. Will the artists appeal to the god-side or the ape-side of the audience's human nature?

Much depends on their choices and their audiences' choices, as the impressions coming into the minds of both the artists and their audiences affect their spiritual vibration. This is not an attempt to preach the virtues of inspirational books and films, and the dangers of horror, pornographic, and violent media. My intent is just to cast light on the choices that we ape-god humans face, and the consequences of our choices.

We all have talents and skills that we can use in this world for better or for worse—in the interests of our god-side or our ape-side.

Willis Harman, late president of the Institute of Noetic Sciences, once told me that the biggest changes in history don't happen when a few leaders make big decisions; they happen when a *lot* of people change their minds a little bit. That is the strategy of this book: To try to help change a lot of minds a little bit. If I believed we could sweep the ape-side of our nature off the planet and bring paradise to this world, I'd be preaching with tremendous zeal. As it is, I realize that the best we can do in today's world is to chip away at the situation—to educate ourselves about our mixed heritage, to encourage each other to foster our god-side, and to respect those among us who can do that.

My life mission and afterlife mission have become clear to me in recent years: After I die, I plan to get settled into paradise, and then, working with colleagues on earth, participate in missions to lower worlds to bring people home to paradise. At the same time, I'll work on the ITC project to open the communication channels between earth and the finer levels of spirit.

At least, that's my current plan. Our spirit friends have told us that once we die, everything changes. Many preconceived notions fly out the window, life over there being so different from what we on earth can conceive.

Developing such projects involving focused collaboration between heaven and earth will depend on far greater interest and understanding here on earth than what is present today. Most people have little genuine spiritual understanding. They have no interest whatsoever in spiritual communication and redemption of lost souls. ITC and a spiritual cleansing of the world can't happen without widespread human interest in things spiritual. Everything else is in place for world ITC—the technology on our side, and the interest and the technology on the other side of the veil.

So my purpose now, before I die, is to get lots of people on earth excited about our rich spiritual heritage in general, and about the ITC project and soul redemption work in particular. I'm working with colleagues in various parts of the world to create fertile ground for mankind's future spiritual growth. I'm using my writing skills more than anything else, since that's what I was blessed with in this lifetime.

What is your mission? What can you do to make the world a better place? If you don't already know your life purpose, assess your talents, skills, and desires, then answer that question. Then take that first bold step. Goethe once wrote a great couplet:

> If there's something you can do, or dream you can, begin it. Boldness has genius, power and magic in it.

Beyond that simple formula, there are a few other things we can do to stay on track.

Foster self-knowledge. What's bold to someone else might not be bold to us. Our purpose might be to become the secretary-general of the United Nations, or it might be to teach, in which case it might involve teaching our family. Or our purpose might be to live life like an angel—to join with someone else in marriage or in partnership in order to help them stay on track, to tame their wild side, to encourage wholesome choices, to inspire them, and so on—as they focus the bulk of their energy on their creative purposes of helping the world. Our purpose in this case is to provide guidance, support, and inspiration, in the same way that finer spiritual beings help individuals on Earth.

Keep our day job. Some people are lucky enough to be aligned to their mission, and are making money doing it, but most of us are not. For those of us involved in a job that's not particularly fulfilling, it's best not to discard our livelihood right away. Most of us need an income as we set off in search of our mission. Unless we have a wealthy benefactor, a huge nest egg, or an incredibly supportive and understanding spouse, we'll probably want to keep our job at first, and then phase it out as our new purpose-driven livelihood evolves.

Stay active. If we keep taking steps toward our goal, we keep moving in the right direction. If we become preoccupied by diversions and forget the goal, the momentum stops. So stay active. Connecting with other people who are active and compatible can move us all toward our goals more quickly. It should not be a chore to stay on task with your purpose, it should be an inner urge that pulls you forward. If it's a chore, then you might be on the wrong path.

Embrace opportunities, resist temptations. Genuine opportunities can help us. Temptations can hurt us. If we can learn to discern between the two, the path to our goal opens up. The more on-purpose we become, the more opportunities and the fewer temptations come our way.

Learn from mistakes. Learn from other people's mistakes, as well as our own.

If we're already doing all these things and we're making the world a better place, then we're probably fulfilling our purpose and completing our mission, even if we're not fully aware of exactly what that mission is. The more we stay on-task, the clearer our mission becomes.

Few things on earth are more gratifying than knowing our purpose for being here and being aligned to that purpose. Our spirit friends have told us that between lifetimes our spiritual self assesses the progress we've made during our incarnations on earth, and we chart a purpose or mission for the next lifetime. As a result, we're born into this world with a rich spiritual heritage and an intimate familiarity of our purpose.

It would be nice if we could hold onto that spiritual insight as we grow into a toddler, an adolescent, and finally an adult. We could know our purpose throughout our life and stay on task. Unfortunately life on earth doesn't work that way. These physical bodies are rugged vehicles designed to operate in the rugged earthly environment. Once we're born, our brain soon becomes inundated with the lights, colors, sounds, fragrances, and flavors of the physical world flowing through our physical senses, and by the age of three or four the higher, nonphysical senses have closed down for most of us.

When we are young, a protective cloak develops between our mind and spirit, blocking out negative spiritual influences that can disrupt our vulnerable mind. Later on in life that cloak can be carefully removed through spiritual practice, allowing us to perceive beyond the physical world. When our higher senses are activated in appropriate ways, we can see and hear into the finer worlds of spirit. We can see smiling faces and beautiful places, we can hear inspiring voices and music that fills the heart, we can get insights and impressions from brilliant nonphysical minds beyond the earth, and we can become channels for powerful healing energies that can trigger miraculous healings in people. And most important, we can tune in to our own, personal soul mission—our purpose for being here on earth at this time.

We can do a little soul-searching to determine whether or not we're ready to know our purpose. Are we ready to pursue our mission? Are we completely at peace with our life, or is there a certain restlessness within us—a sense that there's something more we should be doing? If we feel an inner restlessness, then perhaps it's time to begin moving into our life purpose.

AFTERWORD

The Seven ethereal beings have come close to our world for the seventh time. They are here today, observing the choices we make in the coming years. It is a crucial time. They have tried to enlighten humanity through six civilizations in the course of thousands of years. They started with Shanidar of prehistoric times, then chose Babylon, then three other civilizations, and most recently (I believe) the nation and religion of Israel in biblical times. Who will they choose today? Who will be the next chosen people? Will it be:

- The Christians, who have spread biblical miracles and teachings to mankind?
- The Americans, whose proud heritage of freedom and innovation provided most of the modern technologies that have brought humanity together more closely today than ever before possible?
- Western-world citizens in general, nations in North America, Europe, and the Pacific Rim who have embraced and improved upon the technologies to become part of the emerging global brain?

- The Muslims, who strive to protect themselves—by religion when possible, by force when necessary—from the spreading moral decay and oil addiction of the West?
- The Chinese, who have become masters of long-range social planning and population control?
- The Hindus, with their rich spiritual heritage?
- The South Americans, especially Brazilians, in whose cultures the veil between heaven and earth is especially thin?
- The Buddhists, who choose a path of peace and detachment from worldly trappings and believe that enlightenment is the path to end suffering?
- The Africans, who have born the heaviest burden of human suffering?

You've probably figured it out by now: It's all of humanity. Modern communication technologies make it possible today, for the first time in history, for all of mankind to unite. With phones and computers and satellites and other devices we can have a meeting of people from almost anywhere in the world, at anytime. We've broken the constraints of space and distance, a condition that brings us one step closer to paradise on earth.

All we have to do now is to iron out our incompatibilities, heal our inequities, and foster effective, humane social systems that will strive perpetually to find that workable balance between individuals' needs for freedom and societies' needs for stability. That's a big order, but I know it's do-able with knowledge of our true spiritual nature, and with foresight and fortitude to envision a bold, beautiful future for ourselves and for our world.

I believe it has been the hope of the ethereal beings—God's plan, The Project—to open communication bridges to all of humanity, an awakened humanity that is aware of its ancient spiritual heritage and willing to fulfill its destiny to create and preserve paradise on earth. Through these open bridges to ethereal realms, light, love, and wisdom of the ages will stream into our world, lifting mankind to a new level of enlightenment. Paradise will be restored.

Ethereal beings are ready and waiting for us to make these choices, and when we do, ITC bridges will open wide. How do I know? They told us, verbatim, in English, through an ITC system in Europe:

> This is the seventh time that we accompany and guide you on your progress toward a free, wealthy, and sane future in which humanity would have stripped off the chains of intolerance and cruelty—a future in which it will be able to establish fruitful, endurable relationship with the light, ethereal realms of existence.[29]

It doesn't get much clearer than that—a message coming through a recording device directly from ethereal minds for whom thousands of years on earth pass by in a heartbeat. A pure and perfect message from the subtlest, most brilliant realms, unfiltered by any human mind.

I hope you feel as inspired by our prospects as I do. The writing is on the wall, and the message is one of hope: If we humans try to make the right decisions in the coming years at the personal, community, national, and global levels, we will begin building a bridge to paradise.

---

[29] Excerpt of a contact from The Seven received August 22, 1996, through the telephone-answering device of Maggy Harsch-Fishbach. The message came a few weeks before our second annual INIT meeting. I arranged the meeting in Tarrytown, New York, which I'm sure is part of the reason the message was in English, and also why Harsch-Fishback was obliged to give me that recording on the first day of the meeting.

ABOUT THE AUTHOR

Mark Macy has explored matters beyond science and written about them most of his adult life. After a stint in Vietnam with the Navy, he spent the seventies as an agnostic, developing a systems approach to world affairs (*Solutions for a Troubled World* and *Healing the World and Me*), and caroming in the nineties into technical spiritual research after nearly dying from colon cancer (*Conversations Beyond the Light* and *Miracles in the Storm*). He founded an international panel in 1995 to explore and foster a young field of research involving direct communication with the other side through technology, and he has been immersed ever since.

Mark lives with his wife, Regina, in his native Colorado, where they like to hike and ski a few times a year in the Rockies, of which they have a majestic view from their window. Their son, Aaron, is in college.